Poverty and Ecclesiology

Nineteenth-Century Evangelicals in the Light of Liberation Theology

Justo L. González
Anthony L. Dunnavant
William C. Kostlevy
Bill J. Leonard
Donald W. Dayton

Anthony L. Dunnavant
Editor

A Michael Glazier Book
THE LITURGICAL PRESS
Collegeville, Minnesota

A Michael Glazier Book published by The Liturgical Press

Cover design by David Manahan, O.S.B.
Cover photograph courtesy of Paynesville Historical Society, Paynesville, Minnesota.

1   2   3   4   5   6   7   8   9

Library of Congress Cataloging-in-Publication Data

Poverty and ecclesiology : nineteenth-century evangelicals in the
    light of liberation theology / Justo L. González . . . [et al.].
        p.   cm.
    "A Michael Glazier book."
    Includes bibliographical references.
    ISBN 0-8146-5024-4
    1. Church work with the poor—History. 2. Evangelicalism—United
States—History—19th century. 3. Liberation theology.
    I. González, Justo L.
    BV639.P6P684 1992
    261.8'325'09—dc20   92-18818
                                                                    CIP

Contents

Contributors

JUSTO L. GONZÁLEZ is director of the Hispanic Summer Program of the Fund for Theological Education and editor of the Journal of Hispanic Theology *Apuntes*, as well as of the *Comentario Bíblico Hispanoamericano*. A graduate of Union Theological Seminary in Cuba (S.T.B.) and of Yale University (S.T.M., M.A., Ph.D.), he is the author of many books including *A History of Christian Thought*, *The Story of Christianity*, *Faith and Wealth*, and *Mañana: Christian Theology from a Hispanic Perspective*.

ANTHONY L. DUNNAVANT is associate professor of church history at Lexington Theological Seminary in Lexington, Kentucky. A graduate of Fairmont State College (B.A.), West Virginia University (M.A.), and Vanderbilt University (M.Div., M.A., Ph.D.), he is the editor of the *Lexington Theological Quarterly* and a contributor to *A Case Study of Mainstream Protestantism: The Disciples' Relation to American Culture, 1880–1989* (ed. D. Newell Williams).

WILLIAM C. KOSTLEVY is special collections librarian of the B. L. Fisher Library at Asbury Theological Seminary in Wilmore, Kentucky. A graduate of Asbury College (A.B.), Marquette University (M.A.), Bethany Theological Seminary (M.A.Th.), and the University of Notre Dame (M.A.), he has contributed to *The Brethren Encyclopedia* and *Methodist History*.

BILL J. LEONARD is chair and professor in the department of religion and philosophy at Samford University in Birmingham, Alabama. A graduate of Texas Wesleyan College (B.A.), Southwestern Baptist Theological Seminary (M.Div.), and Boston University (Ph.D.), he is the author of *The Nature of the Church* and *"God's Last and Only Hope": The Fragmentation of the Southern Baptist Convention*. He is a frequent contributor to *The Christian Century*.

DONALD W. DAYTON is professor of theology and ethics at Northern Baptist Theological Seminary in Lombard, Illinois. A graduate of Houghton College (B.A.), Yale Divinity School (B.D.), the University of Kentucky (M.S.), and the University of Chicago (Ph.D.), he is the author of *Discovering An Evangelical Heritage* and *Theological Roots of Pentecostalism*. Professor Dayton edited "The Higher Christian Life: Sources for the Study of the Holiness, Pentecostal and Keswick Movements, 1830–1920," and, with Robert Johnston, *The Variety of American Evangelicalism*.

Introduction

The quest for Christian unity has been a conspicuous feature of the Church's life in the twentieth century. The persistence of division in the Body of Christ, however, has been equally visible. In churches in the United States in the late twentieth century intradenominational polarization is at least as potent and rancorous as interdenominational discord. Many of the latter divisions are, in fact, alienations within denominational families—among various kinds of Methodists, or of Baptists, or of the churches of the Stone-Campbell heritage.

In the midst of estrangement, there are tenuous expressions of unity among churches with closely shared histories. For example, among the Stone-Campbell churches (the Christian Church [Disciples of Christ], the undenominational fellowship of Christian Churches and Churches of Christ, and the Churches of Christ), the activity of the Disciples of Christ Historical Society is one such expression. The Historical Society serves and is supported by all three churches. It was at a Society event, the Forrest F. Reed Lectures for 1986, that I heard Churches of Christ scholar Richard Hughes discuss David Lipscomb, one of the primary leaders of the Churches of Christ (the group often seen as the "right wing" of the Stone-Campbell movement). Hughes spoke of Lipscomb's "bias in favor of the common people" and of Lipscomb's conviction that the true "church of Christ was a church by, of, and for the common people."* Such phrases seemed strikingly similar to those used by liberation theologians. The liberationists' usage of such language is taken seriously in the theological reflections of

---

*Richard T. Hughes, "The Editor-Bishop: David Lipscomb and the *Gospel Advocate*," in *The Power of the Press: Studies of the Gospel Advocate, the Christian Standard and The Christian-Evangelist*, by Richard T. Hughes, Henry E. Webb, and Howard E. Short, The Forrest F. Reed Lectures for 1986 (Nashville: Disciples of Christ Historical Society, 1987) 26.

mainline Christians. How did these ideas fit into the ministry of someone as notoriously "non-mainline" as David Lipscomb?

The labels "mainline" and "evangelical" convey a host of associations, but none of these associations is more familiar than that of "mainline" with the advocacy of social action and of "evangelical" with an emphasis on personal piety. Operating within such a framework, mainline Christians in North America would be expected to have a sympathetic interest in Latin American liberation theologies with their social and political engagement. This interest has, in fact, emerged and has generated a whole range of issues and questions for mainline Christians.

Richard Hughes' claims about Lipscomb, however, raised a different set of questions. What about the "conservative" Christians? Does the emergence of liberation theology have anything to do with evangelical readings of the Christian tradition? Why is it that North American mainline Protestants seem so receptive to the insights of Latin American liberationists, at least from a distance, and yet have seen so little value in similar-sounding views from the evangelical branches of their own denominational family trees? These questions and the underlying ecumenical quest frame the agenda for this book.

The title, *Poverty and Ecclesiology: Nineteenth-Century Evangelicals in the Light of Liberation Theology*, is intended to signify a reflection that brings some of the insights and basic vocabulary of recent liberation theology into dialogue with the views of several nineteenth-century North American Protestants conventionally regarded as religiously conservative. Of course, labels are highly problematic. This is especially so in a book that proposes, in part, to loosen the grip of some familiar ones. "Evangelical" is an obvious example. In order to communicate a very general ethos and rough location on the religious landscape, the term may be defensibly applied to each of the nineteenth-century groups considered. Free Methodists would probably wear that label most easily. Some among the Churches of Christ and Baptist Old Landmarkers, however, would have their distinctive reservations about being so identified. Donald Dayton makes a case for the term "radical" in his Epilogue, but that is a case best made at the end of this work.

This volume begins with an essay in which Justo González sketches the roots of recent Latin American expressions of the "option for the poor" and describes their relationship to the "base communities" that have emerged in that context. This sets the framework for three case studies that examine the views on poverty or ecclesiology of the nineteenth-century founding figures of three North American Protestant groups.

The first case study investigates, along the trajectory suggested by Hughes' brief remarks in his 1986 lecture, the views of David Lipscomb on the church and the poor. Lipscomb's ideas are compared to those of Latin American liberationists. The conventional description of the Churches of Christ as the most conservative group in the Stone-Campbell heritage is given credibility by its early leaders' opposition to "innovations" and insistence on strict adherence to what they understood to be the "restored" faith and practice of the New Testament. Yet one such "conservative" leader, David Lipscomb, articulates a kind of "option for the poor."

In the second case study, William Kostlevy focuses upon B. T. Roberts and the early Free Methodists. Kostlevy establishes the "evangelical credentials" of the Free Methodists in terms of their long and prominent relationship with the National Association of Evangelicals. He also recounts the group's origins in Roberts' perception that the Methodist Episcopal Church was compromising its historic Wesleyan heritage ethically and doctrinally. B. T. Roberts' decrying of "New School Methodism" was similar to Lipscomb's condemnation of "progressive" elements in his community. But Roberts, too, is found to express an "option for the poor."

The third case study shifts the focus away from the "option for the poor" as such to the closely related issue of ecclesiology. Bill J. Leonard compares the recent *comunidades eclesiales de base* with the autonomous local churches of the Baptist Old Landmarkers. As in the instance of the Churches of Christ, the Old Landmarkers have been renowned for their "conservatism." Do the views of their first-generation leaders J. M. Pendleton and J. R. Graves have anything in common with those of recent liberationists? Leonard finds in both a "radical reassertion of the importance of the local congregation and the role of the people as a source of authority and ministry for the whole Church."

These essays each acknowledge profound differences in the historical settings and specific development of the ideas on poverty and ecclesiology of the Christian leaders considered. But in spite of these differences, there are significant similarities in the views of these nineteenth-century North American and twentieth-century Latin American Christians. A common accent on the poor or on a more grassroots, locally contextualized, understanding of Church resonates among these communities.

This, then, is partially a book of historical theology. It is also a plea for the recovery of a kind of "family memory." Taken together, the three case studies touch the denominational families of a considerable portion of American Protestantism: the Stone-Campbell churches, Methodists, and Baptists. It is hoped that readers across the spectrum of these divided families will consider afresh the elements of their own heritages highlighted here. It is also an invitation to see the ecumenical possibilities that may lie beyond the boundaries of familiar definitions of liberals, liberationists, Catholics, and conservative or evangelical Protestants.

Anthony L. Dunnavant
Lexington Theological Seminary

Chapter One

The Option for the Poor in Latin American Liberation Theology

Justo L. González

Historical background

The phrase "preferential option for the poor" has been correctly identified with Latin American liberation theology. Yet the notion itself, far from being an invention of Latin American liberation theology, has a long history which encompasses many of the earliest Christian writers,[1] much of medieval tradition,[2] and even such revered saints of the Protestant tradition as John Wesley.[3]

In Latin America, the struggle on behalf of the poor, and theological reflection in the midst of that struggle, began almost as soon as the conquest itself. In 1511, after significant deliberation among the Dominicans in Hispaniola, Antonio de Montesinos went before the Spanish settlers and preached a sermon to which his colleagues had agreed:

> In order to make your sins known to you I have mounted this
> pulpit, I who am the voice of Christ crying in the wilderness of this

[1]Numerous references may be found in a study which I concluded recently: *Faith and Wealth: A History of Early Christian Ideas on the Origin, Significance, and Use of Money* (San Francisco: Harper & Row Publishers, 1990).

[2]Including the acrimonious debates regarding "evangelical poverty" which took place in the University of Paris in the thirteenth century, and the struggle in the later centuries of the Middle Ages to reform the Church by making it again a poor Church. An interesting and illuminating study of one aspect of this struggle is Lester K. Little, *Religious Poverty and the Profit Economy in Medieval Europe* (Ithaca, NY: Cornell University, 1978). See also Michel Mollat, *The Poor in the Middle Ages* (New Haven: Yale University Press, 1986).

[3]See Theodore W. Jennings, Jr., *Good News to the Poor: John Wesley's Evangelical Economics* (Nashville: Abingdon, 1990), especially 47–69.

9

island; and therefore it behooves you to listen to me, not with indifference but with all your heart and senses; for this voice will be
the strangest, the harshest and hardest, the most terrifying that you
ever heard or expected to hear. This voice declares that you are in
mortal sin, and live and die therein by reason of the cruelty and tyranny that you practice on these innocent people. Tell me, by what
right do you wage such detestable wars on these people who lived
mildly and peacefully in their own lands, where you have consumed
infinite numbers of them with unheard-of murders and desolations?
Why do you so greatly oppress and fatigue them, not giving them
enough to eat or caring for them when they fall ill from excessive
labors, so that they die or rather are slain by you, so that you may
extract and acquire gold every day? And what care do you take that
they receive religious instruction and come to know their God and
creator, or that they be baptized, hear mass, or observe holidays
and Sundays?

Are they not men [*sic*]? Do they not have rational souls? Are you
not bound to love them as you love yourselves? How can you lie
in such profound and lethargic slumber? Be sure that in your present
state you can no more be saved than the Moors or Turks who do not
have and do not want the faith of Jesus Christ.[4]

This was the beginning of a long line of protest against exploitation, and of solidarity with the exploited. The work of Bartolomé
de Las Casas is well known, and it is not necessary to review it here.
He spent his entire life protesting against the violence being done
to the native inhabitants of the Western hemisphere, seeking the
enactment of laws prohibiting such violence, and living among the
natives, trying to show that his preachment of an "alternative conquest" of love was practicable. His fame is such that many believe
he was a lone crusader against universal indifference. Yet that was
not the case. On the contrary, there were many who took a similar
stance. The Dominicans and other friars in Chile, following the
leadership of Gil González de San Nicolás, declared that wars against
the natives in order to take their lands and possessions were unjust. He and the other friars on the colony decided that those who
profited from such wars could receive no absolution until they made
restitution.[5] Although González was silenced, his views and work

[4]Quoted in H. McKennie Goodpasture, ed., *Cross and Sword: An Eyewitness History of Christianity in Latin America* (Maryknoll, NY: Orbis Books, 1989) 11–12.

[5]Fernando Mires, *La colonización de las almas: Misión y conquista de América* (San José: Departamento Ecuménico de Investigaciones, 1987) 68–70.

were later taken up by the Jesuit Luis de Valdivia.[6] The story of the Jesuit missions in Paraguay, and their resistance to encroaching forces of slavery, has been popularized in the movie *The Mission*. If anything, the movie does not show the degree to which the Jesuits carried their support for their Guaraní converts—to the point of helping them make weapons and organize an army for their self-defense. St. Luis Beltrán, the first of the missionaries to the Western hemisphere to be canonized, was outspoken in his defense of the natives. One of the miracles attributed to him in his canonization process took place when Beltrán was sitting at the table of an *encomendero*.[7] His host took offense at Beltrán's comment that the Spanish were living off Indian blood. To prove his point, Beltrán took a tortilla and squeezed blood from it. Furthermore, most of these people were not isolated defenders of the natives, but rather formed part of a vast network which kept in touch through correspondence and other means.

I have pointed out elsewhere[8] that these early "voices of compassion" shared three characteristics that make them forerunners of present-day liberation theologians: their concern and passion were born out of the experience of solidarity with the poor; they went beyond protest to plans for political and other action; they based their action on a reinterpretation of Scripture and its application to their situation. What I meant by the first of these characteristics is very similar to what is meant by the "preferential option for the poor." These were people, mostly Dominican friars, whose religious vows of poverty made it possible for them to approach the imposed poverty and oppression of their native flock with a spirit of solidarity. Where those who sought after riches saw only progress and an empire being built, these friars, many of whom actually lived among the native population, saw families being destroyed, civilizations being wiped out, and in general, as several said on occasion, Christ himself being blasphemed, not by their supposedly "pagan" charges, but by the "Christian" colonizers.

[6]Ibid., 70–79.
[7]The *encomiendas*—trusts—were a system whereby a Spanish trustee—*encomendero*—would receive a number of natives "in trust," in order to teach them the Christian faith. In exchange, the natives were expected to work for their keep. Obviously, this was a system open to much abuse, which usually led to the natives being treated worse than slaves.
[8]In "Voices of Compassion," *Missiology* 20 (April, 1992) 163–73.

At a later time, others rose to the similar challenge posed by black slavery. Late in the sixteenth century, San Martín de Porres, himself the son of a black woman and a Spaniard who later became Governor of Panama, became known for his compassion, not only for the sick and the poor, but also for sick and hungry animals. It was, however, St. Peter Claver, a Jesuit, who became most famous in his advocacy for the oppressed—particularly slaves and poor freed blacks. His "preferential option for the poor" was both obvious and offensive to many. One of his biographers declares:

> The attitude of a Jesuit who devoted almost his whole life to the negroes and actually seemed to prefer their company to that of the whites was regarded by some of his fellows not only as an oddity but as an affront. . . . "While there were negroes about," records Brother Nicolás, "it was useless to attempt to confess to Claver. After the slaves came the poor, and when they were lacking, the children from the school." Another witness, a lady prominent in Cartagena society, states that, "he loved the negroes so much that he was loath to confess Spaniards, and if any Spaniard asked him for his confession, he would answer that the negroes were in great poverty, that they had masters to serve, whilst the Spanish ladies never lacked for confessors ready at their call; and in any case, he was fit only for blacks."[9]

Thus, the "preferential option for the poor" has a long history in Latin America, and is not properly understood when it is seen as the brainchild of liberation theologians, inspired by Marxist ideas. While many liberation theologians have used Marxist economic and social analysis to try to discover and to lay bare the causes of poverty in Latin America, the option for the poor is much older than any such analysis.

Official Pronouncements: Vatican II, Medellín, and Puebla

A month before the opening session of the Second Vatican Council, Pope John XXIII preached a sermon in which he declared: "As it faces the underdeveloped countries, the Church presents itself as it is and wishes to be, as the Church of all, and particularly

[9]Stephen Clissold, *The Saints of South America* (London: Charles Knight & Co., 1972) 187–88.

the Church of the poor."[10] This statement expressed concerns that had been voiced by a number of Church leaders throughout the world, particularly after the Second World War. It also gave further impetus to those who thought that the poor and their plight should be a major concern of the Church.[11] At the first session of the Council, Cardinal Lercaro, Archbishop of Bologna, took up the Pope's directive and argued that "the Church of the poor" should be the main concern of the Council. At a series of meetings, and through lectures and publications of such distinguished theologians as Marie-Dominique Chenu and Yves Congar, an informal group was organized around the theme of "the Church of the poor."

Circumstances surrounding the Council were ripe for such a debate. Only 42 percent of the bishops represented the churches of Europe and English-speaking North America, while 46 percent came from Asia, Africa, and Latin America. More than half came from churches so poor that they could not defray all the expenses of their representatives at the Council, and had to rely on support from the rest of the Church. Furthermore, the Second Vatican Council had been convoked with a very open agenda, and without a specific heresy or concrete threat to crystallize its concerns, and therefore it was free to respond to agendas such as the "Church of the poor," brought to the foreground by the pastoral concerns of the prelates present. In general, the mood of the Council was not one of simply approving what the Curia and its commissions had prepared beforehand, but rather one of making sure that subjects were thoroughly discussed by those present, and that the final documents did indeed represent their views—this, to such a point that not a single document was adopted as written by the preparatory commissions, and almost all were radically rewritten.

In spite of all this, the documents of Vatican II did not satisfy those who most eagerly wished for the Church to take a prophetic

---

[10]*L'Osservatore romano,* Sept. 12, 1962: "In faccia ai paesi sottosviluppati la Chiesa si presenta quale é, e vuol essere, come la Chiesa di tutti, e particolarmente la Chiesa dei poveri."

[11]The story of these conversations surrounding the Council is well summarized in Julio Lois, *Teología de la liberación: Opción por los pobres* (San José: Departamento Ecuménico de Investigaciones, 1986) 11–23. This includes a summary of Lercaro's speech, as well as the story of the group that organized around the theme of "the Church of the poor."

stance in favor of the poor, and against the root causes of poverty. Much of what it said, although calling for the Church to pay special attention to the poor, was rather ecclesiocentric and even condescending. Thus, in the Dogmatic Constitution on the Church, the Council declared:

> Just as Christ carried out the work of redemption in poverty and under oppression, so the Church is called to follow the same path in communicating to men [*sic*] the fruits of salvation. . . . Thus, although the Church needs human resources to carry out her mission, she is not set up to seek earthly glory, but to proclaim humility and self-sacrifice, even by her own example.
>
> Christ was sent by the Father "to bring good news to the poor, to heal the contrite of heart (Lk. 4:18), to seek and to save what was lost" (Lk. 19:10). Similarly, the Church encompasses with love all those who are afflicted with human weakness. Indeed, she recognizes in the poor and the suffering the likeness of her poor and suffering Founder. She does all she can to relieve their need and in them she strives to serve Christ.[12]

And, in an even more disappointing way, the same document seems to imply that the poor ought to be content with their lot, for this comes from God and brings them closer to Christ:

> Those who are oppressed by poverty, infirmity, sickness, or various other hardships, as well as those who suffer persecution for justice's sake—may they all know that in a special way they are united with the suffering Christ for the salvation of the world. The Lord called them blessed in His gospel. . . .
>
> All of Christ's faithful, therefore, whatever be the conditions, duties, and circumstances of their lives, will grow in holiness day by day through these very situations, if they accept all of them with faith from the hand of their heavenly Father.[13]

The one place in which the preferential option for the poor is most clearly expressed in the documents of the Council is in the Decree on the Ministry and Life of Priests, which says that "although he has obligations toward all men [*sic*], a priest has the poor

---

[12]Second Vatican Council, Dogmatic Constitution on the Church, 21 November 1964, 8.

[13]Ibid., 41.

and the lowly entrusted to him in a special way."[14] Yet, as one reads further one realizes that this is only one among many such "special obligations"—which include youth, married people, parents, etc. There is also a similar injunction to the bishops, although with no explanation as to what it might entail.[15]

It is in the Pastoral Constitution on the Church in the Modern World, commonly known as *Gaudium et spes,* that the Council made the statements that would most profoundly affect Latin American liberation theology. The document itself had not even been anticipated by the planning commissions, but was rather the result of the insistence of the Council to speak on a number of crucial issues in modern life. For that reason, it was a more spontaneous, less ecclesiocentric document than most others that the Council produced. The statements in that document which provided an impetus for liberation theology had to do, not so much with the preferential option for the poor, as with an existing economic order which produces and increases poverty. In this document, the Council acknowledged that, although the development of economic life in the modern world is such that it could diminish social inequalities,

> . . . yet all too often it serves only to intensify the inequalities. In some places it even results in a decline in the social status of the weak and in contempt for the poor.
>
> While an enormous mass of people still lack the absolute necessities of life, some, even in less advanced countries, live sumptuously or squander wealth. Luxury and misery rub shoulders. While the few enjoy very great freedom of choice, the many are deprived of almost all possibility of acting on their own initiative and responsibility, and often subsist in living and working conditions unworthy of human beings.[16]

In a clear rejection both of laissez-faire liberal capitalism, and of state socialism, the Council declared that "theories that obstruct the necessary reforms in the name of a false liberty must be branded as erroneous. The same is true of those theories which subordinate

[14]Second Vatican Council, Decree on the Ministry and Life of Priests, 7 December 1965, 6.

[15]Second Vatican Council, Decree on the Bishops' Pastoral Office in the Church, 28 October 1965, 13.

[16]Second Vatican Council, Pastoral Constitution on the Church in the Modern World, 7 December 1965, 63.

the basic rights of individual persons and groups to the collective organization of production."[17] And, in a strong statement of the rights of the poor, the document went on to declare that "the right to have a share of earthly goods sufficient for oneself and one's family belongs to everyone. . . . If a person is in extreme necessity, he [*sic*] has the right to take from the riches of others what he himself needs."[18]

Finally, the Council affirmed the rights and value of private property, but then went on to limit such rights and to address the situation of the impoverished nations of the world. Since this text has been very influential in the thought of Latin American liberation theologians, it is worthy of extensive quotation:

> By its very nature, private property has a social quality deriving from the law of the communal purpose of earthly goods. If this social quality is overlooked, property often becomes an occasion of greed and of serious disturbances. Thus, to those who attack the concept of private property, pretext is given for calling the right itself into question.
>
> In many underdeveloped areas there are large or even gigantic rural estates which are only moderately cultivated or lie completely idle for the sake of profit. At the same time the majority of the people are either without land or have only very small holdings, and there is evident and urgent need to increase land productivity.
>
> It is not rare for those who are hired to work for the landowners, or who till a portion of the land as tenants, to receive a wage or income unworthy of human beings, to lack decent housing, and to be exploited by middlemen. Deprived of all security, they live under such personal servitude that almost every opportunity for acting on their own initiative and responsibility is denied to them, and all advancement in human culture and all sharing in social and political life are ruled out.
>
> Depending on circumstances, therefore, reforms must be instituted if income is to grow, working conditions improve, job security increase, and an incentive to working on one's own initiative be provided. Indeed, insufficiently cultivated estates should be distributed to those who can make these lands fruitful. In this case, the necessary ways and means, especially educational aids and the right facilities for cooperative organization, must be supplied. Still, whenever the common good requires expropriation, compensation

[17]Ibid., 65.
[18]Ibid., 69.

must be reckoned in equity after all the circumstances have been weighed.[19]

While all of this shows a growing concern for the poor, and the text last quoted begins to take into account the structures and systems which make people and nations poor, much of it was ecclesiocentric. The poor themselves were not the center of concern, but rather the object for which and through which the Church was to show its concern for justice. The poor were seen as receiving the ministries of the Church, and even as profiting from its advocacy, but not as agents in the cause of justice or the ministries of the Church.

While those in Latin America—and elsewhere—who hoped that the Council would speak decisively on issues concerning the poor and poverty were disappointed, the Council nevertheless gave them leave and even encouragement to continue their work. In Latin America, it was a time of grave social and economic crisis. The Alliance for Progress had failed to bring about any noticeable improvement in the life of the masses. On the contrary, the living conditions of the poorest continued to decline, and the number of the poor increased rapidly. The apparent economic progress of previous decades had been due in part to the Second World War, and in part to loans which were coming due, and many of which could only be renewed at exorbitant rates of interest. These events led many to give up on "developmentalist" theories, and to seek for different explanations of the poverty which was rampant on the continent, and new solutions to it.

By the time the Second General Conference of Latin American Bishops met in Medellín, Colombia, in August of 1968, it was clear that a much more radical analysis of the Latin American situation was needed, and that from such an analysis would emerge a new way of understanding the mission of the Church. Thus, Medellín would speak with greater clarity regarding the plight of the poor and its causes. It would also base this on an understanding of the gospel which places such issues at its very heart:

> The Latin American Church has a message for all men [*sic*] on this continent who "hunger and thirst after justice." The very God who creates men in his image and likeness, creates the "earth and

[19]Ibid., 71.

all that is in it for the use of all men and all nations, in such a way that created goods can reach all in a more just manner" [Vatican II, Church in the Modern World, 69], and gives them power to transform and perfect the world in solidarity. It is the same God who, in the fullness of time, sends his Son in the flesh, so that He might liberate all men from the slavery to which sin has subjected them: hunger, misery, oppression and ignorance, in a word, that injustice and hatred which have their origin in human selfishness.[20]

On the basis of this understanding of the gospel, and of the human predicament to which it responds, the bishops gathered in Medellín analyzed the economic and social condition of Latin America, and made it quite clear that they understood poverty as primarily the result of unjust structures and economic systems. While they did not propose a socio-economic program or blueprint, they did reject both Marxist communism and liberal capitalism:

> The system of liberal capitalism and the temptation of the Marxist system would appear to exhaust the possibilities of transforming the economic structures of our continent. Both systems militate against the dignity of the human person. One takes for granted the primacy of capital, its power and its discriminatory utilization in the function of profit-making. The other, although it ideologically supports a kind of humanism, is more concerned with collective man [*sic*], and in practice becomes a totalitarian concentration of state power. We must denounce the fact that Latin America sees itself caught between these two options and remains dependent on one or the other of the centers of power which control its economy.[21]

On this basis, Medellín made a rather exhaustive and damning analysis of the situation of Latin America, and even of the manner in which the Church had allowed itself to be perceived as either rich or at least allied to the interests of the rich.[22]

[20]Second General Conference of Latin American Bishops, *The Church in the Present-Day Transformation of Latin America in the Light of the Council* (2d ed; Washington, D.C.: USCC, 1973), "Justice," 3.

[21]Ibid., 10.

[22]The document is careful to say, not that the Church or its prelates are inordinately rich, but that they have allowed that impression to remain, partly through secretive bookkeeping practices, partly through their policies vis-à-vis the various classes in society, and partly because it is true that some have lived in luxury and ostentation.

Medellín, however, went further. It no longer saw the poor as the object of charity or of concern on the part of the Church. It also realized that if a more just economic order is to emerge this will take place only if means are found to counteract the influence of the elites which hold power to their own advantage. For this reason, the Conference proposed a plan to develop the political consciousness of the people, but above all it called for the multiplication of "small basic communities":

> It is necessary that small basic communities be developed in order to establish a balance with minority groups, which are the groups in power. This is only possible through vitalization of these very communities by means of the natural innate elements of the environment.[23]

What is significant about this declaration is that, although Medellín did not use that language, what is being proposed here is that the poor become subjects, rather than objects, of their own history. It is no longer only a matter of the Church advocating on behalf of the poor, or sharing their plight, as had been proposed in Vatican II. Naturally, that was expected to continue. What was now added was a program placing the poor at the very center of political, economic and ecclesiastical action. Although "basic Christian communities" already existed when the bishops met at Medellín, the Conference recognized and even promoted their political power, and decided that their formation was to be encouraged precisely for that reason.

The decisions and statements made at Medellín gave further impetus to a number of theologians who, even before Vatican II, were searching for ways in which the Church and its message could be more relevant to the Latin American situation. It was mostly after Medellín that these theologians began exploring the meaning of the "preferential option for the poor," not only in political and ecclesial praxis, but also in theology.

Thus, by the time the bishops of Latin America met again in a general conference, this time in Puebla, Mexico, in 1979, the "option for the poor" and the liberation theology which undergirded it had become both widespread and controversial. There were even concerted efforts to rally major donors in opposition to liber-

[23]Ibid., 20.

ation theology, and specifically against the "preferential option for the poor." Yet the bishops stood firm, reiterating and even strengthening what had been declared earlier at Medellín:

> With renewed hope in the life-giving power of the Spirit, the III Latin American Conference takes again the position of the Conference of Medellín, which made a clear and prophetic option of preference and solidarity for and with the poor, and this in spite of the distortions and interpretations with which some twisted the spirit of Medellín, and the scorn and even hostility of others.[24]

Even though many had criticized the decisions of Medellín, and the theology of liberation which those decisions supported, Puebla made it very clear that the bishops of Latin America had decided that there was no return from the position of Medellín, nor from the "preferential option for the poor." Therefore, it may be said that Puebla made such an option the official stance of the Catholic Church in Latin America, although even after Puebla there have been repeated efforts to bring that Church to a more conservative stance.[25]

A Preferential Option for the Poor

Although most of the elements involved in the phrase, "preferential option for the poor," appear long before that time, the phrase itself, and its many variants, do not appear in Latin American liberation theology until the decade of the seventies. Gustavo Gutiérrez apparently employed it for the first time in a lecture delivered in El Escorial, Spain, in 1972.[26] After that time it has been used with increased frequency by liberation theologians, to the point that it has come to take the place of earlier phrases

---

[24]Conferencia del Episcopado Latinoamericano, *Documentos de Puebla* (Madrid: PPC, 1979) 319.

[25]The pressures from the Vatican have been many, and need not be discussed here in detail. A number of theologians and other Church leaders have been silenced. The organization of Latin American bishops itself has been captured by more conservative elements. The Vatican has issued two "instructions" against liberation theology. In more recent times, misunderstanding the role of Marxism in that theology, many have expressed the hope that, with the demise of communism, liberation theology will also disappear. None of these measures has been able to suppress what is clearly the most significant theological development in the five hundred years during which Christianity has been present in Latin America.

[26]Lois, *Teología de la liberación: Opción por los pobres*, p. 336, n. 112.

such as "liberating praxis," as perhaps the central axis around which most Latin American liberation theology revolves. As Leonardo and Clodovis Boff have said,

> One can understand liberation theology as the faith-reflection of a church that has taken seriously the preferential option of solidarity with the poor. Starting from them and with them, the church wishes to act in a liberating fashion. This option is not self-seeking or political, as if by it the church were seeking to place itself alongside the outstanding historical force of our time: the popular classes, which are ever more decisive in the course of history. The church does this rather by virtue of its own proper motivations, which are inherent to Christian faith itself.[27]

If one is to understand liberation theology itself, one must understand the meaning of the preferential option for the poor. To opt for the poor does not mean simply to be concerned for them, to offer them help, or to seek better economic conditions for them. Nor does it mean simply to become poor, or to spend time among the poor. All of these things may be good and even necessary; but the preferential option for the poor is more than that. To opt for the poor means to opt for a struggle with the poor and on their behalf. Even those who are poor, in the sense of having no possessions, must make an option for the poor, in the sense of deciding to join the poor in their struggle for justice.[28]

It is important to understand this point, for it is here that middle-class Christians are tempted to fall into the old trap of paternalism and call it an "option for the poor." What is required of middle-class people is not that they decide to help the poor. What is required is that they come to understand the pain of the poor and the reasons that make them poor, and that they then cast their lot, not into helping the poor through charity or the like, but into the struggle for a different social order.

Thus, everyone, from the richest to the poorest, is called to make an option for the poor. Naturally, this will take different forms depending on one's station in life, for while the rich must divest them-

[27]Leonardo and Clodovis Boff, *Cómo hacer teología de la liberación* (Madrid: Ediciones Paulinas, 1986) 60.

[28]As Lois has put it, "mere material poverty does not produce, *ex opere operato*, the option for the poor. The need for conversion implied in the option is universal in its scope." *Teología de la liberación*, p. 417, n. 15.

selves so as to be able to experience solidarity with the poor, no such divestment is required of the poor. But in every case the option for the poor takes on the nature of a conversion in which the entire shape and order of the world is changed.

This conversion is necessary, not only for individuals, but also for groups and for the Church itself. As the Puebla Conference put it,

> In order to live and to announce the demands of Christian poverty, the entire church must revise its structures and the life of all its members, especially of its pastoral agents, seeking an effective conversion. Thus converted, the church will be able to evangelize the poor effectively.
>
> This conversion involves the demand for an austere lifestyle and a total trust in the Lord, for in this evangelizing action the church will have to trust more on the being and the power of God and of divine grace than on its own having more or on secular power. Thus will the church project an image which will be truly poor, open to God and to the brother or sister, always available, in which the poor are really able to participate and are acknowledged in their worth.[29]

Furthermore, the option for the poor involves partisan action, taking sides on behalf of the poor and their struggle. If the analysis of the causes of poverty which lies at the root of liberation theology is correct, then it is impossible to make an option for the poor without making an option against the structures and the interests that cause poverty. According to this analysis, poverty is not the result of ignorance, sloth or fate, but of systems and structures that make some people poor and others rich. Thus the way to fight poverty is not simply to increase production—although there is nothing necessarily wrong with such increase—but to improve distribution. As a result, an option for the poor will necessarily be an option against structural injustice, and by extension against the interests of those who profit from such injustice—normally, although not exclusively, the rich.

Sin, as liberation theology understands it, takes historical shape—although not exclusively—in oppression and injustice. Likewise, salvation takes historical shape in liberation from injustice and from oppression. Oppression is a denial of God's love and truth.

---

[29] *Documentos de Puebla*, 324–25.

Liberation is an affirmation and a proclamation of God's love and truth.

> This is how we bring to pass the truth of God at the very heart of a society in which social classes confront one another with hostility. For we shall be taking sides with the poor, with the populous classes, with the ethnic groups others scorn, with cultures that are marginalized. It is from there that we must strive to live and proclaim the gospel of the love of God. Its proclamation to the exploited, to the laborers and *campesinos* of our lands, will lead them to perceive that their situation is contrary to the will of the God who makes himself known in events of liberation. It will help them come to a consciousness of the profound injustice of their situation.[30]

This involves not only a political conversion, but also an epistemological one. We are used to reading history and all of reality, so to speak, "from above," that is, from the perspective of the powerful, the conquerors, those who have control not only over the means of production, but also over the means of interpretation. The conversion to the poor, the option for the poor, leads to an entirely different reading of history and of reality. From the perspective of the powerful, for instance, the European invasion of the Western hemisphere, which began five hundred years ago, was a glorious process of conquest, evangelization and civilization. But from the perspective of the poor in Latin America, who are mostly descendants of the original inhabitants of these lands, the invasion has brought ever increasing poverty and suffering. In the United States, from the perspective of those whose taxes were cut and whose income increased, the Reagan years were the best in recent history. Not so from the perspective of those, mostly poor, whose income declined while their taxes remained constant or even increased. From the perspective of Pharaoh, it is a beautiful city that is being built. From the perspective of the children of Israel, things appear altogether different. To make a preferential option for the poor is to take the side of the poor, not only in the sense of joining in their struggle, but also in the sense of viewing reality and history from their viewpoint.

This, however, does not mean that a mere naive reading of history suffices. This is so because the means of interpretation have

---

[30]Gustavo Gutiérrez, *The Power of the Poor in History: Selected Writings*, Robert R. Barr, trans. (Maryknoll, NY: Orbis, 1983) 18.

been placed at the disposal of the existing order to such an extent that even the poor have often come to believe an interpretation which places on them the blame for their own victimization. For this reason, the conversion to the poor must also entail the application of new instruments of analysis, and the development of a new perspective which will be able to place the blame for injustice and oppression where it really belongs. This is one more reason why even the poor have to be "converted to the poor." From this conversion one is able to see poverty, not as the result of vice or sloth, nor as the result of ignorance or backwardness—as when one speaks of "underdeveloped" nations—but rather as the result of oppression.[31]

On the other hand, this does not mean that even the most sophisticated economic analysis can substitute for the experience of the poor themselves. One cannot make an "option for the poor" by deciding what is good for the poor in the absence of the poor. Even though the poor do not have the means for social analysis, they have the experience which, once affirmed and unleashed, can provide many an insight into the world as it really is—that is, as it is when seen "from below."

For this reason, the preferential option for the poor involves providing spaces where the poor can be empowered to interpret the world as they see it, and affirmed in their intuitions "from below." This is one of the functions of the "Christian base communities"—*comunidades eclesiales de base*—which have played and continue to play such an important role in Latin American liberation theology.

These Christian base communities are small groups of believers who gather periodically, usually to pray, to study Scripture, and to discuss how their faith relates to the situations in which they live. Most of them are organized in the neighborhoods where people live, but others are organized where they work, study, etc. The manner in which their meetings are conducted varies greatly; but the main principle is that all are encouraged to speak, and that people's experience and insight are respected and affirmed. As has been stated above, these "base communities" were promoted after Medellín, as a way to develop groups that would counterbalance the power of elites. However, they have also functioned as centers

---

[31]Boff, *Cómo hacer teología de la liberación*, 36–40.

where the "Church of the poor" has become a reality, and where the poor have once more claimed the Bible for themselves.

At this point it may be helpful to clarify that the common English translation of their name, "Christian base communities," leaves out an important dimension in the Spanish name, *comunidades eclesiales de base*—as well as in the similar Portuguese name. These are not just groups that get together; they have an *ecclesial* nature. They are the Church existing in the community. Yet, they are not *ecclesiastical;* they are not churches, nor do they pretend to be. Although in many cases such communities clash with the institutional Church, their purpose is not to serve as substitutes for the Church and its sacraments, but to make them more relevant to the situations in which people live, partly through biblical and theological reflection, and partly through concerted action.

In order to understand the importance of the communities for biblical interpretation, it is necessary to remember that until recently the Bible itself was relatively little known among the rank and file of Roman Catholicism in Latin America. People knew the general outline of the gospel, and of Christian doctrine, but very seldom had they had the opportunity to read Scripture itself. Thus, when they now come to study and discuss the Bible in a base community, they do so with surprising freshness. They do not know what they are supposed or expected to find in the Bible, and therefore they come up with surprising finds—finds which, once pointed out, seem obvious to any reader, but which we have missed because we have not been provided with the opportunity to read Scripture "from below."[32]

This is what liberation theologians call "the epistemological advantage of the poor." Surprisingly, the poor are able to understand things which the non-poor do not. If it is true that Jesus came to preach "good news to the poor," it follows that the poor will have an easier time understanding the gospel than the non-poor. And, if most of the Bible was written from a perspective of poverty, oppression, and persecution, it follows that those who read it from

[32]Probably the most widespread book in which North American readers have encountered this naive, yet very profound reading of Scripture is the four volumes by Ernesto Cardenal on *The Gospel in Solentiname,* Donald W. Walsh, trans. (Maryknoll, NY: Orbis, 1976). Discussing the gospel reading for the day, a group of peasants and fisherfolk in a village in Lake Managua discover surprising riches in the biblical text.

a similar perspective will understand it more readily and more correctly than those who read it from a perspective of power, security, and comfort.

In this sense, the "preferential option for the poor" is also an option for the God whose Word comes to us most clearly when mediated through the experience and struggles of the poor.

Conclusion

In summary, the option for the poor has a long history in Latin American Christianity. From its earliest manifestations, long before the phrase itself appeared, it involved living in solidarity with the poor, acting on their behalf in order to change oppressive political and economic structures, and a different view of theology and Scripture. In more recent times, thanks to the new openness provided by the Second Vatican Council, and to the follow-up work done in Latin America, it has led to an entire rediscovery of the meaning of Scripture, as well as to a reinterpretation of history and of present-day realities—particularly economic and political realities. As such, it has also opened the way to a new interpretation of the life of the Church, centered now on small base communities where people live out their faith, analyze their situation, and plan and coordinate strategies of liberation.

Chapter Two

David Lipscomb and the "Preferential Option for the Poor" Among Post-Bellum Churches of Christ

Anthony L. Dunnavant

In the quarter-century since the Second General Conference of the Latin American Episcopal Council in Medellín, Columbia, the theme of a "preferential option for the poor" has become increasingly familiar in the theological discourse of Christians. However, part of the power of this idea is rooted in its claim to great antiquity within—and even beyond—the Christian tradition. The Catholic bishops at Medellín likened their discernment of God's presence in "the present-day transformation of Latin America" to that of "Israel of old," which "felt the saving presence of God" when God "delivered them from the oppression of Egypt by the passage through the sea and led them to the promised land."[1] In a similar fashion, when the Latin American Episcopal Council met in Puebla in 1979, its document on "A Preferential Option for the Poor" drew from both the ancient tradition of the people of God and the more immediate past. From the ancient past it invoked images of "the poor of Yahweh," the poor Christ, the Jesus who evangelizes the poor, the Mary of Magnificat, and the "evangeli-

[1]Second General Conference of Latin American Bishops, *The Church in the Present-Day Transformation of Latin America in the Light of the Council*, vol. 2: *Conclusions* (2nd ed.; Washington, D.C.: Division for Latin American—USCC, 1973) 33, 36.

cal poverty'' of the gospels and the First Epistle to Timothy. But the immediate past of the ''rise of grassroots communities'' was also foundational to the document.[2] This kind of historical consciousness, one that is both deep-rooted and attentive to the contemporary scene, is characteristic of much Latin American Catholic theology, certainly of that associated with ''liberation.''[3]

As Robert McAfee Brown describes it, part of the challenge to North American Protestants that the Latin American statement of ''a preferential option for the poor'' presents is that this option is a ''vocation that will appeal only to those few North American counterparts'' of the grassroots Church communities. Both the historical orientation of liberation theology and Brown's suggestion raise the possibility that within the stream of North American Christianity there might be traditions—or at least individuals—that have embodied or expressed ''a preferential option for the poor.'' Furthermore, as North American Protestants seek ways to ''embrace the notion,'' they might be helped by a recognition that the notion is neither entirely new nor entirely alien to the Christian tradition in their own cultural heritage. *This is not to suggest, of course, that the theological, social, historical, and cultural differences between North America and Latin America may be simply swept aside. Those differences are profound.* It is to suggest that those moments and movements that share a certain resonance of emphasis and insight might fruitfully be identified.[4]

[2]John Eagleson and Philip Scharper, eds., *Puebla and Beyond: Documentation and Commentary,* John Drury, trans. (Maryknoll, NY: Orbis Books, 1979) 264–66. As my quotation from these episcopal documents indicates, I am defining ''Latin American Catholic liberation theology'' loosely enough to include both the Medellín *Conclusions* and the Puebla document on ''A Preferential Option for the Poor'' within its orbit. The association of the Medellín conference with liberation theology is, I think, quite defensible. The case for making the same association with the Puebla conference is weaker. However, I will draw mainly from Puebla's ''Preferential Option'' document, which has been interpreted by liberationists as in essential continuity with Medellín (see Gustavo Gutiérrez, *The Power of the Poor in History,* Robert R. Barr, trans. [Maryknoll, NY: Orbis Books, 1983] 125–65). The ''grassroots communities'' mentioned here are the *comunidades eclesiales de base.* These are also called ''base Christian communities,'' ''basic ecclesial communities,'' ''Grass-roots church communities,'' etc.

[3]See, e.g., Gutiérrez, *Power of the Poor in History,* especially 3–22.

[4]Robert McAfee Brown, ''The Significance of Puebla for the Protestant Churches in North America,'' in Eagleson and Scharper, *Puebla and Beyond,* 343. Elsewhere Brown himself has identified aspects of the ''national song'' of the United States that might be in harmony with the ''key'' of liberation theology. His examples

It is in this spirit of striving to identify other discoveries of God's concern for the poor that we turn to the North America of the nineteenth century and the Campbell-Stone movement. This movement emerged on the western frontier of the United States in the early national period. In it are the roots of three major North American religious bodies, the Christian Church (Disciples of Christ), the undenominational fellowship of Christian Churches and Churches of Christ, and the Churches of Christ. It was in the closing years of the nineteenth and opening years of the twentieth centuries that the Campbell-Stone community divided. The division that produced the Churches of Christ as a distinctive body was rooted, at least in part, in a socioeconomic bifurcation in the movement. That Churches of Christ represented, during the generation after the Civil War, *much more* than the other branch of the movement a "religion of the disinherited" is suggested by both the actual wealth of congregations and the perspective of the group's leadership.[5] Clearly, Churches of Christ *saw themselves* as relatively materially poorer than their former religious compatriots. The time and place that the Churches of Christ arose gives credence to this self-image.[6] Within the Campbell-Stone movement, then, the focus will narrow to Churches of Christ between the Civil War and World War I. This was a period in which this group was—*relatively* and in self-perception—poor. Further, the focus will be on David Lipscomb, who was one of the principal leaders of this group, and on ways in which he approached articulating a "preferential option for the poor."

David Lipscomb is the figure most strongly associated with the emergence of the Churches of Christ as a distinct religious com-

reflect, for the most part, harmony on the central theme of socioeconomic and political liberation. I have chosen, in this work, to pursue similarities of focus that arise in the eccesiastical and biblical (texts and themes) arenas more narrowly construed. (*Theology in a New Key: Responding to Liberation Themes* [Philadelphia: The Westminster Press, 1978] 143–46).

[5]David Edwin Harrell, Jr., *A Social History of the Disciples of Christ*, vol. 1: *Quest for a Christian America: The Disciples of Christ and American Society to 1866* (Nashville: The Disciples of Christ Historical Society, 1966) 79.

[6]It has also been argued, in quite a different context, that "relative poverty may be more significant socially than absolute poverty" (Caroline Hodges Persell, *Understanding Society: An Introduction to Sociology* [New York: Harper & Row, 1984] 255). See also, note 8 below; David Edwin Harrell, Jr., *A Social History of the Disciples of Christ*, vol. 2: *The Social Sources of Division in the Disciples of Christ 1865–1900* (Atlanta and Athens, GA: Publishing Systems, Inc., 1973) 334–40.

munity within the larger Campbell-Stone movement. It was around his views as expressed in the *Gospel Advocate* during the two generations between the Civil War and World War I that the Churches of Christ "consolidated."[7] The fact that this religious body has been, and remains, overwhelmingly, a people of the southern United States is important to an understanding of Lipscomb. It was the southern strand of the Campbell-Stone movement that came closer to being identified with the "disinherited" than the other strands. Richard T. Hughes has recently suggested that Lipscomb was "not only . . . a man of God and a man of the book [the Bible], but also . . . a man of his region and a man of the people." This, then, is the first aspect of Lipscomb's views that resonates with the Latin American "commitment to solidarity with the poor, to being a church of the poor"—a simple identification with the poor, or the "common masses."[8]

---

[7] Earl Irvin West, *The Life and Times of David Lipscomb* (Henderson, TN: Religious Book Service, 1954) 7; on the importance of Lipscomb, see also Robert Eugene Hooper, *A Call to Remember* (Nashville: Gospel Advocate Company, 1977) 31.

[8] Richard T. Hughes, "The Editor-Bishop: David Lipscomb and the *Gospel Advocate,*" in *The Power of the Press: Studies of the Gospel Advocate, the Christian Standard and The Christian-Evangelist,* by Richard T. Hughes, Henry E. Webb, and Howard E. Short, The Forrest F. Reed Lectures for 1986 (Nashville: The Disciples of Christ Historical Society, 1987) 23. I am indebted to Professor Hughes for alerting me to Lipscomb's general identification with the common people. The same theme is treated in some detail in the chapter, "The Cry of the Poor," in Robert E. Hooper's work, *Crying in the Wilderness: A Biography of David Lipscomb* (Nashville: David Lipscomb College, 1979) 222–34. On the current geographic distribution of the Churches of Christ, see Wade Clark Roof and William McKinney, *American Religion: Its Changing Shape and Future* (New Brunswick and London: Rutgers University Press, 1987) 312, 136.

Part of Lipscomb's rhetoric about the poor and especially about the laborer must be seen in the context of that of the "greenbackers and freesilverites of the middle and late 1870s" and of the Populists of the 1890s. As was the case for Lipscomb to some degree, in the writings of these groups, "the primacy of producers . . . was a constantly recurring idea" (Walter T. K. Nugent, *From Centennial to World War: American Society 1876–1917,* The History of American Society, ed. Jack P. Green [Indianapolis: The Bobbs-Merrill Company, Inc., 1977] 101).

The regional identification of David Lipscomb is an important point relative to his perspective on poverty. Although there is considerable controversy surrounding the causes of poverty in the southern United States in the years between the Civil War and World War I, there is little doubt of the *fact* of poverty in that region in those years. Harold D. Woodman has provided a good review of the diverse economic-historical interpretations of the post-Civil War South in "Sequel to Slavery: The New History Views the Postbellum South," *The Journal of Southern History*

David Lipscomb's views share other significant similarities with those arising from the orbit of Latin American Catholic liberation theology. Lipscomb's concern for the poor was not vague, abstract, or ahistorical. Like liberation theology, which is based on "concrete historical and political conditions," David Lipscomb's writings about the poor were based on his own personal experience of poverty in the concrete historical situation of the Civil War and Reconstruction-era southern United States. He understood this poverty as having both regional and economic (as opposed to *merely* individual and moral) dimensions.[9] Early in 1866 Lipscomb wrote:

63 (4 [November 1977]) 523–54. Woodman observes that "the masses of white population who never owned slaves were . . . undergoing a momentous process of social change for which they had little experience. Hill-country whites, who had been largely self-sufficient yeomen, were being transformed into commercial farmers. Like the former slaves [white yeomen] borrowed from local merchants to whom they gave crop liens, but they also secured their loans with mortgages on their lands. In the process, many lost their lands and came to occupy a status little different from that of the blacks" (552). In the years between the Civil War and World War I, there emerged "a special southern form of wage laborer" based on "share wages" and a resurrected form of the plantation modeled after the "large-scale, thoroughly capitalistic farm." The working class, "divided by racial antagonisms, failed to cooperate either in unions or in lasting political alliances." Furthermore, "disenfranchisement laws prevented political activity by virtually all the black and large sections of the poor white population. Planter capitalists, along with merchants and textile and other manufacturers enjoyed a kind of unfettered capitalism . . . The majority of the population—and hence the South as a whole—remained poor" (553). Even if one rejects Woodman's analysis, the fact of poverty in the post-Civil War South remains clear. The interpretation of Robert Higgs, for example, which sets out to correct "exaggerated" accounts of the "problems of Southern development," nonetheless concedes that "Southern income levels remained substantially below those elsewhere [in the United States] throughout the post-Civil War era." Furthermore, even during the period between 1880 and 1900 when the rate of growth in Southern incomes kept pace with the nation as a whole, "the *absolute* difference between Southern and non-Southern income levels became wider." Despite a narrowing of this gap between 1900 and 1920, Higgs concludes his discussion recognizing a "relative poverty of the South in the post-Civil War era—and indeed right up to the present day" (*The Transformation of the American Economy, 1865-1914: An Essay in Interpretation,* The Wiley Series in American Economic History, Ralph L. Andreano, ed. [New York: John Wiley & Sons, Inc., 1971] 108, 110, 114).

With this perspective, it is perhaps not crucial to distinguish between "the poor" and "the common people." However, David Lipscomb does sometimes make a distinction between "poverty" and "a moderate competence." This is not consistent and Lipscomb uses phrases like "honest, industrious, independent poverty and toil" to represent a kind of ideal (D. L. [David Lipscomb], "Who Are to Blame?" *Gospel Advocate* 11 [May 6, 1869] 422, 425).

[9]Gustavo Gutiérrez, "Liberation Praxis and Christian Faith," *Frontiers of Theology in Latin America,* ed. Rosino Gibellini, trans. John Drury (Maryknoll, New

We have in the South brethren impoverished, and suffering for the necessaries of life, whose misfortune it was to share the general desolation of the country in which they lived. We have brethren North of us who have grown rich by the very circumstances that impoverished our brethren South.[10]

The "general desolation" of the Civil War was the large, historical background which fed Lipscomb's "insatiable desire to help the distressed people of the South."[11] But his experience with poverty was not confined to his efforts to help others who were impoverished. During the Civil War years, poverty had come very close. He reflected in late 1866,

It is but a year or two since we ourselves were in a condition of almost actual starvation. The writer of this has visited, within the last four years, our Senior Editor, who could not give him bread to eat; this was his condition for weeks. . . . We have visited other families that were near to us, in which we felt that every mouth full of food we ate was taken from women and children who must suffer for the want of it.[12]

If Lipscomb's own experience of poverty, perceptions of its causes, and efforts on behalf of the poor "destitute" Christians of the South are seen as one "pole" of his concern, the other "pole" is clearly the example of Christ seen in Scripture. Again, there is a striking similarity with the familiar Christological basis of the Church's option for the poor in the Latin American liberation theology literature. On the one hand, there is the reference to the Jesus of the gospels' claim that "God may be found in the poor" (Matt 25); on the other hand there is the imagery of *kenosis*.[13]

Lipscomb alluded to the first of these themes in the following passage:

Christ is personified in his poor, helpless brethren. Matt. xxv:40. In them, Christ appeals for help to himself. Who realizes this? . . .

York: Orbis Books, 1979), 23; West, *David Lipscomb*, 112–115; Hooper, *Crying in the Wilderness*, 230.

[10]D. L. [David Lipscomb], *Gospel Advocate* 8 (3 [January 16, 1866]) 46.

[11]West, *David Lipscomb*, 114.

[12]D. L. [David Lipscomb], "A Word to Our Southern Brethren," *Gospel Advocate* 8 (48 [November 27, 1866]) 758.

[13]For an expression of these themes from the perspective of liberation theology, see Jon Sobrino, *The True Church and the Poor*, Matthew J. O'Connell, trans. (Maryknoll, New York: Orbis Books, 1984) 152, 150, 137.

Let us realize that every helpless, needy one of our brethren is the personification of Christ to us appealing for help. He is our Christ, to be kindly welcomed and generously treated. Shall we cast our Christ from our doors and let him become a beggar from others? Let us be careful, "Verily I say unto you inasmuch as you have done it unto one of the least of these my brethren, ye have done it unto me." "Inasmuch as ye did it not to one of the least of these ye did it not to me."[14]

He also invoked the image of Christ's self-emptying as the example which calls Christians to sacrificial giving on behalf of "the masses":

Without timely aid, the masses, unable to raise crops the coming year, will be in as bad condition another winter as they have been during the past. . . . It is folly in us to deceive ourselves on this subject. . . . We must sacrifice our luxuries, our comforts, our wealth and pride, to relieve our brother's distresses, just as Christ sacrificed his honors, glories, joys and possessions in heaven, to help poor helpless, fallen man [*sic*] on earth. This was the fellowship of God to man. I will give of my honors and joys to you, and take of your weaknesses, sufferings, and sorrows to myself, is the language of Jesus to man, in his mission to earth. Our fellowship for one another must be of this character. I'll give of my plenty, and partake of your privations and self-denials, is the language of Christian fellowship.[15]

The language of *kenosis* and the apprehension of Christ (God incarnate) personified in the poor "brother" certainly suggests an orientation of the Church "for the poor." But as liberation theologian John Sobrino says, "a church for the poor is not yet a Church *of* the poor." To use Sobrino's language for the question, is there in the writings of David Lipscomb a recognition that "the Church of the poor is a Church the social and historical basis of which is to be found among the poor"? Yes! Lipscomb repeatedly stated his assumption that "the great masses of professed Christians are now, [and] ever we trust will be from the poor, laboring classes."[16] Lipscomb traced the history of the poor people of God in sweeping terms, reminding his readers that God's

[14]D. L. [David Lipscomb], "Aid to Christians in Need—How Shall it be Administered?" *Gospel Advocate* 12 (11 [March 17, 1870]) 253.

[15]D. L., [David Lipscomb], "The Destitution South." *Gospel Advocate* 9 (9 [February 28, 1867]) 171–72.

[16]Sobrino, *The True Church*, 92, 135; D. L. [David Lipscomb], "New Publications," *Gospel Advocate* 8 (1 [January 1, 1866]) 11.

prophets of olden time were poor, often clothed in sackcloth. His
Son was born of an humble handmaid of the Lord, who was es-
poused to a carpenter. The reputed Father of our lord, Joseph, was
a carpenter. The laboring, toiling classes were the associates chosen
of God for his Son during his childhood and youth. The more prominent of his Apostles were from the laboring classes. Several followed
the uncertain and precarious calling of fishermen. *They were the chosen vessels of the Lord in which his spirit dwelt, and through whom it guided
and guides the nations of the earth to God and Heaven.* The poor of this
world were the chosen vessels of mercy, the especially honored and
blessed of God. They, as a class, constitute his elect. They are the
chosen objects of his tender regard and true and faithful love. The
great mass of his true and honored followers, in all ages of the world,
have been, ever must be, from the poor.[17] [emphasis added]

The sentence underscored above moves us into another area of the
"preferential option for the poor" which is echoed in Lipscomb's
writings—the importance of the poor as evange*lists* as well as
evange*lized*.

The bishops meeting at Puebla reflected that "the rise of grass-
roots communities have helped the Church to discover the evangelizing potential of the poor. For the poor challenge the Church
constantly, summoning it to conversion; and many of the poor
incarnate in their lives the evangelical values of solidarity, service,
simplicity, and openness to accepting the gift of God."[18] Interest-
ingly, one of the great controversies of David Lipscomb's life was
related to his opposition to the missionary societies that arose within
the Campbell-Stone movement in the middle of the nineteenth
century.[19] He saw these societies as "concentrat[ing] the authority and power and means of all the Christians and all the churches
in a few persons," who tended to be "chosen . . . for their capacity to raise money." Therefore, his opposition to the societies
was based in part on the conviction that "Christ [would have] never
established a religion among the poor, and committed its propagation especially to them as a class—[and] made them the objects
of his most favored blessing, [if] that [religion] required the con-
centration and management of great sums of money in one mass

---

[17]Lipscomb, "Who Are to Blame?," 422.
[18]Eagleson and Scharper, *Puebla and Beyond*, 265–66.
[19]West, *David Lipscomb*, 130–33.

in order to reach its highest prosperity.''[20] Rather, Lipscomb believed that "the religion of Jesus Christ was adapted to the common people" and that "they are those best fitted to maintain and spread that religion." He thought that churches "manned [*sic*] by the working people, suited to the means and conditions of the working people" would be the "effective instruments under God of perpetuating and spreading the religion of Christ in its purity.''[21] He made quite explicit his assumption that "it is altogether a mistake to think that the poor are to be preached to by the rich." Such a mistaken notion was alien to Lipscomb's belief that "the rich corrupt" the Church.[22]

Lipscomb's belief that the rich corrupt the Church was accompanied by an oft-repeated caution that the movement of which he was a part should not conform to the ways of the rich and thereby be drawn into this corruption. Again, this resembles the concern expressed at the Second General Conference of the Latin American Episcopal Council at Medellín that there was a perception "that the hierarchy, the clergy, the religious are rich and allied with the rich." This concern led to several suggestions including that priests should know "how to assume the realities and the 'sense of the people' in their circumstances and mentality.''[23] The priests were "exhorted" to "give testimony of poverty and detachment from material goods . . . particularly in rural areas and poor neighbor-

[20]David Lipscomb, "Societies and the Gospel Advocate," in *Queries and Answers by David Lipscomb*, J. W. Shepherd, ed. (5th ed.; Nashville, Tennessee: Gospel Advocate Company, 1963) 392; D. L. [David Lipscomb], "Mr. Brown's Article on Interest," *Gospel Advocate* 10 (36 [September 3, 1868]) 841. In contrast to what he viewed as the futility of "devising ways and schemes for raising money to hire men to preach," Lipscomb told the story of Madison Love: "While wise, learned men have been philosophising as to the impracticability of reaching men in the extreme South without a large amount of money, a poor shingle-maker from Tennessee . . . was guided by the hand of God to the extreme southern coast of our land, where, to an honest, simple-hearted people, he spoke the word of life. . . . A human society would never have done this work. Your 'sensible plans' would have sought the chief cities and influential centres, and have squandered money and time in seeking the influential, while God guided his servant to his chosen— the poor. . . . [Love] was not old when he died; he had baptized over five thousand persons with his own hands" (D. L. [David Lipscomb], "Response" [to Thomas Munnell], *Gospel Advocate* 9 [13 March 28, 1867] 250).

[21]D. L. [David Lipscomb], "A Visit to Chattanooga," *Gospel Advocate* 21 (14 [April 3, 1889]) 214.

[22]D. L. [David Lipscomb], "The Churches Across the Mountains," *Gospel Advocate* 39 (1 [January 7, 1897]) 4; Lipscomb, "Visit to Chattanooga," 214.

[23]Second General Conference of Latin American Bishops, *Conclusions,* 188, 180.

hoods" and "encouraged," if they felt so called, "to share the lot of the poor, living with them and even working with their hands."[24]

Similarly, Lipscomb had a special desire that the preaching ministry be not conformed to "the tastes and habits of the rich." He therefore opposed, to some degree, education for the ministry and an itinerant, hired ministry. He maintained that both preachers and other Christians were well-advised to support themselves through manual labor, at least partially.

On the issue of education, Lipscomb observed in 1866 that

> There is just now a great anxiety manifested for an educated ministry. This is all right, if that education is properly conducted, we often-times think that the habits acquired, and the tastes formed, in getting the education, are not such as are most desirable for enabling the preachers to do good service. Our schools, like our churches, are modeled and conducted to suit the tastes and habits of the rich. If a poor young man, by dint of his own energy or by the aid of friends, enters and passes through school, his associations and surroundings are those of the rich. He forms habits and tastes in consonance with these, loses sympathy with the habits and wants of the poor, and is deprived of his power for reaching those whom it is his especial duty to reach and benefit. The poor are those to whom the Christian minister should be prepared and trained to preach.[25]

Lipscomb's argument against an itinerant "hired" ministry sounds similar themes and adds others—including an encouragement to "live poor":

> The whole plan of a Preacher's putting himself up to the highest bidder, shifting about from place to place, for the sake of a little higher salary is at once a degradation to Christianity, demoralizing to the man and the worst of policies for his support. It makes merchandise of the Christian religion, supplying the preaching of the Gospel to the rich because they are rich, leaving the poor destitute because they are poor, thus thwarting the plan of salvation, *for in it the Gospel is to be preached to the poor because they are poor*. This system keeps the Preacher ever in an unsettled and harassed state of mind, which disqualifies him for usefulness. Makes him in all his

---

[24]Ibid., 193.
[25]D. L. [David Lipscomb], "Educated Preachers," *Gospel Advocate* 8 (1 [January 1, 1866]) 175.

preaching over anxious to please, which destroys his independence and true self respect. . . .

When the brethren aid you, be thankful and preach the Gospel, when they neglect you, work, and toil and preach the Gospel. Don't grumble or complain. *Don't seek the rich and honorable to preach to, but preach to the poor, the neglected, the degraded, and if you live poor you will have the respect of the good and true, your own self-approval, and better than all, the approval of your Father in Heaven. You will be one of the world's true heroes and Heaven's crowned victors.*[26] [emphasis added]

Elsewhere David Lipscomb makes clear that his admonition to "work and toil" includes his assumption that labor with one's hands is to be preferred.[27]

Lipscomb believed that the preference for the poor in evangelism necessitates the Church's maintaining an atmosphere that is not alienating to the poor:

Whatever is introduced into worship in the congregation, either in preaching, singing, praying or biblical reading, that . . . transcends the power of appreciation of the very large majority of the worshippers, and hearers . . . becomes, to use the figure of Paul, the veriest barbarism to that class of people to whom the Gospel was especially adapted and sent—the poor.[28]

Three other aspects of the "preferential option for the poor" that are associated with recent Latin American theology are at least implicit in the writings of David Lipscomb. The first of these is what has been called the "epistemological privilege of the poor," the second is service to the poor as the "privileged gauge of our

---

[26]Lipscomb, *Gospel Advocate* 8:47.

[27]D. L. [David Lipscomb], "What Callings are Proper for Christians," *Gospel Advocate* 11 (6 [February 11, 1869]) 122. Lipscomb's view of Scripture convinced him of "a preference of the Holy Spirit for those [callings] which require physical, muscular toil." Even though he admitted that the more important point was that work must be honest and an influence for good, he nonetheless thought it "a sad omen for the religious and moral well-being of a church or community, to see a general disposition to avoid the callings demanding manual labor" (ibid.). Lipscomb did not abandon this thesis. A generation later he wrote: "Manual labor is the labor taught in the Bible. Study, thought, and learning are desirable and helpful in directing manual labor; but the labor is the important thing for the healthy development and well-being of the man [*sic*], morally, mentally, and physically. . . . The laboring man and woman constitute the foundation (D. L. [David Lipscomb], "Manual Labor Good for Man," *Gospel Advocate* 66 [49 (December 3, 1904)] 777).

[28]Lipscomb, "New Publications," 11.

following of Christ," and the third is the vocation of the Church to be "herself bound to material poverty."[29]

"The epistemological privilege of the poor" is a phrase that has been used by Latin American liberation theologians to indicate "that the conditions of oppression endured by the poor make them more open to the liberating word of God than are those who stand in the way of liberation."[30] In other words, "the poor are accepted as constituting the primary recipients of the Good News and, therefore, as having an inherent capacity to understand it 'better' than anyone else."[31] Intimations of this view have already been seen in Lipscomb, who urged preachers to

> not only preach to the poor in public, but in private also. . . . Visit them at their houses, learn to appreciate their trials and difficulties, . . . and school [your]selves to a full sympathy with their condition. Don't be afraid of being troublesome to the poor. *No class of persons will be more benefitted by your conversation and association, or will more cheerfully be troubled with your presence.* . . . [Christ] associated with and made himself one of the poor. His servants should act as he did.[32] [emphasis added]

While this may fall short of being a full statement of an "epistemological privilege of the poor," it does seem to imply more openness on their part to the preacher and, indirectly, more openness to the gospel among the poor. Lipscomb thought of the capacity of the poor, or at least of the common people, as being that of

> men and women of strong, native, discriminating minds and sterling, honest hearts, who have learned what of language they know chiefly from the simple style of the Bible, and that in every day use among the laboring classes of our community.[33]

[29]The first phrase is, according to Deane William Ferm, Hugh Assmann's (*Third World Liberation Theologies: An Introductory Survey* [Maryknoll, NY: Orbis Books, 1986] 33); the second phrase is from the Puebla document, "A Preferential Option for the Poor" (Eagleson and Scharper, *Puebla and Beyond,* 265); the third is from the Medellín conference (Second General Conference of Latin American Bishops, *Conclusions,* 190).

[30]Ferm, *Third World Liberation Theologies,* 33.

[31]Sobrino, *The True Church,* 140.

[32]D. L. [David Lipscomb], *Gospel Advocate* 8 (9 [February 27, 1866]) 142.

[33]Lipscomb, "New Publications," 11.

So convinced was Lipscomb that the poor were fully capable (*preferentially* capable) of understanding the gospel, that in theological education his

> interest [was] in seeing schools adapted to the wants of the poor, at which the humble and unpretending can be educated, without separating them, in habits and sympathy, from the poor, and in which they will be taught the principles and practices of the Christian religion in the fullness of all their parts.[34]

Although it lacks an explicitly sociopolitical liberation context, Lipscomb's language is in accordance with the general idea of a greater "epistemological" and "obediential" capacity of the poor (or at least of the common people) to understand and conform to the gospel. As he wrote, "the common or laboring people . . . are most easily reached, and . . . generally make the best members when converted. . . . [They] have less to hinder their obeying the gospel, and less to hinder service after they obey."[35]

The Catholic bishops at Puebla stated that:

> When we draw near to the poor in order to accompany them and serve them, we are doing what Christ taught us to do when he became our brother, poor like us. Hence, *service to the poor is the privileged, though not the exclusive, gauge of our following of Christ.*[36] [emphasis added]

David Lipscomb's view clearly concurred with the italicized portion of the statement above. On the same issue, Lipscomb's language in the following passage is especially impressive when one remembers how *central* baptism, by immersion, for the remission of sins, is in the conservative strands of the Campbell-Stone movement.

---

[34]D. L. [David Lipscomb], "Our Educational Prospects and Difficulties," *Gospel Advocate* 8 (15 [April 10, 1866]) 235.

[35]Lipscomb, "Churches Across the Mountains," 4. It is clearer that Lipscomb's view does affirm both the "common" person's greater "epistemological" and "obediential" capacities when one bears in mind that, at least in part, the phrase "obeying the gospel" functions idiomatically in Lipscomb's religious community to refer especially to submitting to baptism by immersion upon confession of faith in Jesus Christ. See, for example, David Lipscomb, "What Constitutes Acceptable Obedience," in *Salvation from Sin*, J. W. Shepherd, ed. (Nashville: Gospel Advocate Company, 1950) 208–30.

[36]Eagleson and Scharper, *Puebla and Beyond*, 265.

The man that can spend money in extending his already broad acres, while his brother and his brother's children cry for bread—the woman that can spend money in purchasing a stylish bonnet, an expensive cloak, or a fine dress, merely to appear fashionable, while her sister and her sister's children are shivering with cold and scarce able to cover their nakedness, are no Christians—have not a promise of a single blessing from God; *and notwithstanding they have been baptized for the remission of sins,* may be unremitted in their attendance upon the appointments of the Lord's house, and constant and regular in their family devotions—yet they are on the broad road that leads to death.[37] [emphasis added]

Alongside his powerful exhortation to material service to the poor stands Lipscomb's insistence, again, that preaching the gospel to the poor is what best embodies the spirit of the Church:

The crowning characteristic of the Christian religion in the esteem of its founder, is that the "poor have the gospel preached to them." The church that fails to exhibit that its first, most important work is to preach the gospel to the poor, has utterly failed to appreciate the true spirit of its mission, and the character of work it was established to perform. . . .

. . .The thousands of the poor in the cities and in the country, must be sought out—preached to—must have congregations whose dress, style, manners and associations will draw them to them, rather than repel them from them, and these congregations, so conforming themselves to the true spirit of the Gospel, and adapting their habits to the necessities of the poor, will alone constitute the Church of Christ.[38]

Lipscomb's last line in the above even seems to suggest that "service to the poor," at least in his sense of preaching to the poor, *is* an *exclusive* "gauge of our following of Christ." This is confirmed by his statement that "the man [*sic*] who refuses to bestow his goods, to sacrifice his conveniences and luxuries in order to relieve the wants of his suffering brethren and sisters, and their helpless orphans, is no Christian man, and has no more chance of Heaven than the veriest infidel in the land."[39]

[37]Lipscomb, "The Destitution South," 172.
[38]D. L. [David Lipscomb], "The Spirit of the Church," *Gospel Advocate* 8 (7 [February 13, 1866]) 107–8.
[39]Lipscomb, "The Destitution South," 171.

Third, the Medellín conference concluded that "a poor Church is herself bound to material poverty."[40] This theme was picked up by the bishops at Puebla who called for a "Church . . . more and more independent of the powers of this world." Such a Church would "rely more on the being and power of God and his grace than on 'having more' and secular authority. In this way it will present an image of being authentically poor."[41] Lipscomb's challenges to congregations relative to the "habits" and styles of their members' dress and of their worship have already been noted. He also opposed concentrating the wealth of the Church in two kinds of "structures"—buildings and societies. He despaired of congregations which committed to the course of erecting elaborate buildings saying, "when I hear of a church setting out to build a fine house, I give that church up. Its usefulness as a church of Christ is at an end."[42] In similar fashion, he saw missionary societies as leading people away from God. His main objection to the societies was that they were, in his view, a "corrupting" modification of the divinely constituted order of the Church.[43] However, Lipscomb was also opposed to what he saw as the societies' tendencies toward oligarchic control by "money-loving men."[44] His preference for a Church "herself bound to material poverty," in some sense, is clear in his 1897 statement that:

> I am fast reaching the conclusion that there is a radical and fundamental difference between the disciples of Christ and the [missionary] society folks. These desire to build up a strong and respectable denomination. To do it they rely on strong and moneyed societies, fine houses, fashionable music, and eloquent speeches, too often devoid of gospel truth. Disciples of Christ do not wish fine houses; they wish people to come to Christ, to be saved by the truth. They

[40]Second General Conference of Latin American Bishops, *Conclusions,* 190.

[41]Eagleson and Scharper, *Puebla and Beyond,* 140, 267.

[42]D. L. [David Lipscomb], "Fine Houses for Worship," *Gospel Advocate* 39 (4 [January 28, 1892]) 52. Compare the following statement by the bishops at Medellín: "Many causes have contributed to create [an] . . . impression of a rich hierarchical Church. The great buildings, the rectories and religious houses that are better than those of the neighbor . . . have been some of those causes" (Second General Conference of Latin American Bishops, *Conclusions,* 188).

[43]D. L. [David Lipscomb], "Human Societies Lead from God," *Gospel Advocate* 50 (49 [December 3, 1908]) 776.

[44]Lipscomb, "Societies and the Gospel Advocate," 392.

do not wish any denomination or party, do not rely upon the favor of the rich or fashionable.[45]

When division became clear and an identifiable religious community commonly called the Churches of Christ emerged as separate from the remainder of the Campbell-Stone movement, it largely followed Lipscomb's lead in repudiating extraparochial Church structures. However, Lipscomb's cautionary words were not simply calling for a fully congregational polity for the Church. He also was concerned about the effects of wealth upon institutions that the Church might in any way sponsor or support. He remarked relative to Bible colleges:

> The rich seldom profess Christianity, and when they do, ninety-nine times out of every hundred their influence is to corrupt the church, lower the standard of morality, and relax all discipline in a church. . . . My memory now fails me of a single preacher that either was rich or set his heart upon being rich, that his usefulness as a preacher was not thereby destroyed. Hundreds are ruined as preachers by riches where one is by poverty. *If riches affect individuals so deleteriously in their religious character, is there not danger of too much wealth having an injurious effect upon a school?*[46] [emphasis added]

In sum, there are several themes that have arisen in the liberation theologies of Latin America in the recent past, and in the episcopal pronouncements that have reflected—to a degree—those theologies, that are similar to pronouncements by David Lipscomb, the principal founder of a significant North American religious community—the Churches of Christ. These themes include: 1) a concern for the poor that is rooted in concrete historical and personal experience, 2) an advocacy of activity on behalf of the poor that has its basis in the teachings of the Jesus of the Gospel (Matthew 25) and in the kenosis of Christ, 3) an assumption that the poor are the fundamental historical basis of the Church, 4) a recognition of the evangelizing power of the poor, 5) an assumption that the poor are especially equipped to receive the gospel, 6) a view that service to the poor is (at least) a "privileged gauge of our following of Christ," and 7) a conviction that the institutional

[45]Lipscomb, "Churches Across the Mountains," 4.
[46]Lipscomb, "Educational Prospects and Difficulties," 233–34.

Church (or institutions of the Church) are challenged to distance itself (themselves) from the corrupting influence of material wealth.

Of course, these common themes may not be taken as evidence that David Lipscomb was a "liberation theologian." For one thing, such a statement would be simply anachronistic. But beyond the differences in historical and cultural context, there are substantive differences between Lipscomb's and the liberationists' understanding of the Church's option for the poor.

For example, Lipscomb stands in contrast to much Latin American liberation theology in his insistence that neither the poor—*nor any Christian*—should engage in political action in order to fundamentally change the social order. He bluntly opposed political revolution:

> The Christian is to pay his [*sic*] taxes, and perform all duties laid upon him by the government, that involve no active support of the government, and that involve no violation of the commands of God and the spirit of the religion of Christ, as a part of his duties to God— as his religious duty. God has so ordained that he must. The cheerful performance of these duties must not depend on the character of government, nor upon his approval or disapproval of the government.
>
> Christians are to be supporters and partisans of none. Quiet submission to the requirements in all things not contrary to the will of God and then a quiet submission but persistent refusal to do the thing commanded, is the part of the Christian. A Christian can engage in active rebellion against no government. Neither active support or participation, nor active opposition.[47]

From the foregoing, it may be concluded that a kind of "passive resistance" might be permissable. But no active participation in political struggles for liberation would be countenanced in such a view. Not only did Lipscomb oppose "active rebellion," but he also was severely critical of those who "despise their own condition, are discontented with their lot, and envy those who are possessed of more of the world's goods." This attitude he characterized as "positive sin" and "a violation of the plain letter of the law of God."[48]

[47]David Lipscomb, *Civil Government: Its Origin, Mission, and Destiny, and the Christian's Relation to It* (Nashville: McQuiddy Printing Co., 1913) 132–33.

[48]Lipscomb also commends the Christian religion for making people happy, "not by changing their lot" but by "making them content in their position." (Lipscomb, "Who Are to Blame?" 425).

Clearly, the language of liberation theologian Gustavo Gutiér-rez with respect to political revolution is in sharp contrast with Lipscomb's. Gutiérrez writes, "Christ's liberation is not restricted to political liberation, but it occurs in historical happenings and liberative political actions. . . . It involves immersion in the political process of revolution, so that from there we may proclaim and live Christ's gratuitous and liberative love."[49] Similarly, the discontent of the poor is not condemned, but rather lifted up in the liberation theology context as one of its fundamental premises—a premise resting on God's discontent with the oppression that creates and sustains poverty. Again, in the words of Gutiérrez: "One must keep in mind that the God of the Bible is a God who not only governs history, but who orientates it in the direction of establishment of justice and right. . . . He is a God who takes sides with the poor and liberates them from slavery and oppression."[50]

The contrast between Lipscomb's identification with "the people" and that of Latin American liberationists may be better understood in connection with Lipscomb's concept of the Church. It is in this context that Lipscomb's rejection of "active" participation in politics may be clarified.

In 1908 Lipscomb stated his longstanding convictions:

> For fifty years I have maintained that the church of God is God's institution through which his children can do and receive all good. I have no reason to turn from this. To turn to and rely on human governments and institutions is to forsake God and to distrust his power to save. . . . The question, then, is: Will the Christian do more to promote and sustain the [moral] sentiment by standing aloof from the political strifes and maintaining high moral and religious sentiment or by entering the political strifes and besmirching his [*sic*] garments and his character by the strifes of political partisanship? [Church historian Johann August Wilhelm] Neander says: "The Christians stood aloof from the state, as a priestly and spiritual race, and Christianity seemed able to influence civil life only in that manner, which it must be confessed is the purest, by practically endeavoring to instill more and more of the holy feeling into the citizens of the state." This is God's way for Christians to influence legislation. I believe it is the best and only way. . . .

[49]Gustavo Gutiérrez, "Liberation Praxis and Christian Faith," 23–24.
[50]Gutiérrez, *Power of the Poor in History*, 7.

Political parties come and go, earthly kingdoms rise and fall; but God remains the same yesterday, today, and forever.[51]

This was Lipscomb's characteristic stance: for Christians, the *Church*, as God's institution, is to be relied on; it is sufficient to work a spiritual revolution in the lives of people that will ultimately affect the social order. Any transformation of society by Christianity will be via the vehicle of the Church. Therefore, a clear conception of the proper role of the Church is necessary. This, of course, was one, if not *the* major focus of the Campbell-Stone movement in the nineteenth century.

Lipscomb was clear as to the Church's tasks and their relative importance:

> The first and highest object in the establishment of the Church of God on earth is . . . the perfection of [members'] own character[s] in Christian purity and holiness.
> . . . The secondary work of the Church. . . was the relieving of the physical ills that afflict humanity—feeding the poor, nursing the sick, caring for the orphan, visiting those that are in prison, and exhibiting a tender sympathy for the bodily ills, sorrows, misfortunes and afflictions of our fellow-creatures. . . . The third design was, "for the edifying or building up of the body of Christ." . . . When the first two objects have been gained . . . but little preaching will be needed to bring them into the Kingdom of God.[52]

---

[51]D. L. [David Lipscomb], "Christians in Politics," *Gospel Advocate* 50 (23 [June 4, 1908]) 361; Lipscomb's approving quotation of Neander is significant: "Neander's conception of the history of the church was that of a divine life gaining increasing control over the lives of men [*sic*]. That life is manifested in individuals. . . . [This conception's] weaknesses were its overemphasis on the influence of individuals and its scanty appreciation of the institutional or corporate life of the church." (Williston Walker and others, *A History of the Christian Church* [4th ed., New York: Charles Scribner's Sons, 1985] 634–35).

[52]D. L. [David Lipscomb], "Objects to be Accomplished by a Church," *Gospel Advocate* 10 (47 [November 19, 1868]) 2007, 2009. It is noteworthy that the ministry to the poor is *not* confined to the poor *of the Church*. See also D. L. [David Lipscomb], "Shall Christians Administer to the Alien?" *Gospel Advocate* 10 (44 [October 29, 1868]) 1049. Lipscomb's attitudes were reflected both in his pacifism during the Civil War and in his recommendations relative to the freed slaves after the Civil War. That is, it was to be through the Church and not through politics that the Black former slaves were to be helped (Hooper, *Call to Remember*, 60–62). Consistent with his overall theology was Lipscomb's view that racial discrimination within the Church was far less tolerable than social and political discrimination (ibid., 62–66).

In other words, the Church should eschew political parties, strife, and active support for or rebellion against governments and attend to its own life of cultivating personal sanctity and of giving humane attention to the afflicted. The foregoing suggests an approach that is primarily focused on the internal life of the Church and on suffering individuals.

While this Church-based (ecclesiocentric) and individualistic orientation is strong in Lipscomb, and although this stands in sharp contrast to Latin American liberationists like Gutiérrez, the contrast should not be overdrawn. Lipscomb did see a role for Christians in the political world:

> While Christians should not engage in political questions and strifes, *they have duties to fulfill with reference to all questions that arise in society*—that is, to stand on the side of right and justice, to study the moral questions that arise in the affairs of the world, and warn as to the principles of right and justice. These, in the end, must prevail; and he [*sic*] who teaches these benefits humanity.[53] [emphasis added]

It was in connection with this duty that Lipscomb himself engaged in some discussion of "political questions."

In the wake of the election of 1896 and its controversy over the gold standard (the election with Bryan's famous "cross of gold" speech), Lipscomb wrote in surprisingly "social" terms about socioeconomic, political polarization and impending class-based violence:

> . . .The recent political contest. . . was the occasion of aligning the laboring people against the capitalists in a political conflict as they had never been before. This question of the money standard may never come up again, *but the alignment and contest of these parties will remain.* Both parties to the conflict have been concentrating their forces for some years past. Capital has been increasing and concentrating in fewer hands, and the capitalists have been growing into a solid body. Labor has been learning to appreciate its importance, and the laborers have been learning their strength and concentrating their power. Neither party has been always just in the conflicts, nor is either likely to be always so in the future. Capital is selfish and overbearing. It has controlled legislation in its behalf

---

[53]D. L. [David Lipscomb], "Some Thoughts Suggested by the Political Contest," *Gospel Advocate* 38 (45 [November 12, 1896]) 724.

and to the injury of the laborer. Jesus Christ taught the dignity and honor of labor. He [*sic*] who would be greatest of all, let him be servant of all. His sympathies were with the poor, the laborer, those humble in station, not with the rich or exalted. *In the end the dignity and honor of labor must prevail and its rights be vindicated.* Those possessed of riches may deal justly and cease to legislate for capital and help labor. That is Christian, and would be wise policy, and would prevent a violent conflict. *If they pursue a selfish course, then a violent convulsion must be the end.*[54] [emphasis added]

According to Robert Hooper, the Civil War was the "catalyst for Lipscomb's thinking" about the relationships between rich and poor and between business and politics that set the trajectory of his thought for the remainder of the century. He arrived at the view that "business interests controlled the politics of the United States." He believed that the "panics" of 1873 and 1893 were caused by the "greed of big business and the power hunger of the trusts." He came to see the American laborer as "enmeshed in a kind of slavery."[55] With this perspective, it is not surprising that "Lipscomb was fully convinced that labor 'combinations' were good and necessary for protection against monopolists and capitalist[s]—'the great oppressors of humanity.' "[56] By the closing decade of the nineteenth century, he had reached the opinion that "money is more and more becoming concentrated in the hands of the wealthy" and "is more and more becoming a controlling element in all the affairs of society." He noted, for example, that "money can thwart justice," and saw the emergence of "mob law" as the natural outcome of such corruption: "As things go now, money accumulates on the one hand, and is overbearing and disregardful of human rights. The unmonied masses combine on the other, and, by mob law, assert their power."[57]

In spite of this "social" analysis, Lipscomb did not conclude that the Church should enter into political contests on the side of the poor or the laboring class. He saw the solution to such problems as going in the opposite direction—not that the Church should

[54]Ibid.
[55]Hooper, *Crying in the Wilderness,* 230–32.
[56]Harrell, *Social History of the Disciples* 2:132.
[57]D. L. [David Lipscomb], "Mob Law," *Gospel Advocate* 34 (22 [June 2, 1892]) 340.

enter into social struggles but rather that those "struggling" should be drawn into the Church. Therefore, Lipscomb's was *not* a concept of "integral liberation" in which God and God's Church are linked to the organized struggle of the oppressed. He did not see that as the vocation of the Church.[58] However, given his doctrine of Church, it is noteworthy that he would recognize "class conflict," acclaim the "rights of labor" as linked to Jesus' teaching, and associate money with injustice.

Another area where Lipscomb's view of the poor contrasts with that of the liberation-oriented Latin American Catholic theologians is in Lipscomb's willingness to make moral distinctions among the poor and assert that:

> There is a species of poverty that has never been honored of God—that is a crime in the sight of God—and that justly deserves to be stamped with disgrace and infamy by men [*sic*]. It is that poverty, want and penury that is brought about by idleness, debauchery and crime.[59]

On the other hand, Lipscomb could make poverty into a kind of virtue. His understanding of poverty was not exclusively as a "spiritual poverty" (as in "the poor in spirit"). He was acquainted, as has been shown, with actual, historical, material poverty. But Lipscomb did promote what has recently been called "another kind of spiritualization: that of calling upon the poor to be satisfied with their state . . . of privilege in God's sight."[60] Of course, this ob-

---

[58]"Integral liberation" has been a controversial term. The understanding of it embraced by Gutiérrez would be that it refers to "the totality and complexity of the liberation process." This includes "economic liberation, social liberation, political liberation, liberation of the human being from all manner of servitude, liberation from sin, and communion with God as the ultimate basis of a human community of brothers and sisters." Gutiérrez sees this understanding of "integral liberation" as underlying the Puebla documents (*Power of the Poor in History*, 144–48).

[59]Lipscomb, "Who Are to Blame?" 422. In spite of this statement, Lipscomb sometimes seemed to have agreed with the position of the bishops at Puebla that "the poor merit preferential attention, whatever may be the moral or personal situation in which they find themselves" (Eagleson and Scharper, *Puebla and Beyond*, 265). See, for example, D. L. [David Lipscomb], "Preaching to the Poor," *Gospel Advocate* 15 (17 [April 24, 1873]) 390–91.

[60]This phrase is from Elsa Tamez. Of course, she was not referring to David Lipscomb but to the general danger of such a spiritualization. For Lipscomb, *both* material poverty (understood not as "destitution" but as a "modest competency") *and* the privilege of the poor in God's sight are idealized ("Good News for the Poor," in *Third World Liberation Theologies: A Reader*, Deane William Ferm, ed. [Maryknoll,

servation must be softened by the reminder that such "spiritualization" did not relieve the Church from service to the poor nor did it imply that the principal basis of the Church was other than the *materially* poor. But it is consistent with Lipscomb's general perspective of not seeing oppression as primarily a social, structural, and *as such* a spiritual problem against which God acts in solidarity with the oppressed *in the world*.

After all, in Lipscomb's view this world was "the world from which God delivered us through Christ."[61] His theology was primarily a "theology of otherworldliness," even though it included a concern for the spiritual transformation of people in this world.[62] This "otherworldliness" is reflected in those areas where the contrast between Lipscomb's and Latin American Catholic liberations' views of the Church and the poor are sharpest—in Lipscomb's aversion to political *action* by Christians (beyond allowable "study" and "warning"), his condemnation of the discontent of the poor, and his moralizing categorization of different "species" of poverty—the "disgraceful" versus the "spiritually" virtuous.

In spite of these very significant differences from much of contemporary liberation theology, and in spite of the radically different social, historical, and cultural contexts from which Lipscomb's and the liberationists' theologies arose, David Lipscomb sounded several themes that are in harmony with the recent call for a "preferential option for the poor." The resonance between Lipscomb's writings on this issue and the contemporary theological concern is sufficient to warrant a fresh examination of, and perhaps reappropriation of these themes by North American Christians who value the heritage of David Lipscomb. This process might contribute to North American efforts to recognize a "preferential option for the poor" within their own cultural and religious heritage and through that recognition move closer to understanding that "option" as it is being advocated globally and ecumenically.[63]

NY: Orbis Books, 1986] 195; Lipscomb, "Who Are To Blame?" 422–24). Gutiérrez's approach to synthesizing material and spiritual understandings of poverty through "solidarity and protest" is most clearly distinguishable from Lipscomb's in the area of "protest" (*Theology of Liberation*, 299–302).

[61]Lipscomb, "Christians in Politics," 361.

[62]Harrell, *Social History of the Disciples*, 2:134.

[63]The writer gratefully acknowledges the assistance of William R. Barr (Professor of Theology), Michael Kinnamon (Dean), and Sharyn Dowd (Associate Profes-

sor of New Testament) of Lexington Theological Seminary in the preparation of this article. This research was presented, in abbreviated form, to both the faculty of Lexington Theological Seminary and the Evangelical Theology group of the American Academy of Religion. The helpful responses of both of these groups are appreciated. Portions of this essay appeared as "David Lipscomb on the Church and the Poor," in *Restoration Quarterly* 33 (Second Quarter 1991) 75–85 and are reprinted here with the permission of the publisher.

Chapter Three

Benjamin Titus Roberts and the "Preferential Option for the Poor" in the Early Free Methodist Church

William C. Kostlevy

They [Free Methodists] believe that their mission is two-fold—to maintain the Bible standard of Christianity, and to preach the gospel to the poor. . . . The provisions of the gospel are for all. The "glad tidings" must be proclaimed to every individual of the human race.

But for whose benefit are special efforts to be put forth? Who must be particularly cared for? Jesus settles this question. "The blind receive their sight, and the lame walk, the lepers are cleansed, and the deaf hear, the dead are raised up," and, as if all this would be insufficient to satisfy John of the validity of his claims, he adds, "and the poor have the gospel preached to them."
—*Doctrines and Discipline of the Free Methodist Church* (1903)

The recent emergence of liberation theology has served as a powerful reminder of the deep biblical roots of concern for the poor throughout Christian history. As the above quotation suggests, some of liberation theology's themes, such as the preferential option for the poor, have historical antecedents among North American evangelicals. This does not mean that liberation theology and North American evangelical variations on the theme of the preference for the poor are identical. Profound historical, cultural, and economic differences separate the nineteenth century American evangelical experience and the milieu in which contemporary Latin American theologies of liberation have arisen. Nevertheless, certain similarities cannot and should not be ignored. The tradition of the "preferential option for the poor" in evangelicalism has been obscured by a tendency to caricature evangelicals as individualistic, otherworldly, anti-intellectual, moralistic, and politically withdrawn. This caricature would appear to be confirmed by the fact that many current evangelicals are suspicious of manifestations of modern Christianity such as liberation theology. It seems that neither liberation theologians nor evangelicals are inclined to recognize the common elements in their traditions.[1]

The early history of the Free Methodist Church, particularly as expressed in the life and words of its founder Benjamin Titus Roberts, provides a paradigm of the evangelical expression of the "preferential option for the poor." An examination of this paradigm will demonstrate that, like proponents of liberation theology, the Free Methodist Church was involved with the lives of the economically dispossessed.

Few would question the evangelical credentials of the Free Methodist Church. It was a founding denomination of the National Association of Evangelicals (NAE); Free Methodist bishop Leslie R. Marston, the denomination's most important leader in the twentieth century, served as the NAE's second president; Free Methodist Clyde Taylor represented the NAE on Capitol Hill. In addition, in contrast to the common caricatures of evangelicals as described above, the Free Methodist Church has had a continu-

[1] The involvement of the Free Methodist Church in the lives of the poor has parallels in a number of other evangelical denominations and institutions. Especially relevant for the antebellum period are the abolitionist and feminist concerns of the Wesleyan Methodist Church, the Free Will Baptist Church, Oberlin College, and Wheaton College. In the post war era, the ministries of the Salvation Army and the related American Rescue Workers and Volunteers of America were deeply rooted in the lives of the poor. The publicity-conscious Salvation Army has frequently been treated as a manifestation of the social gospel. This characterization is not inaccurate. However, it does need to be complemented with the observation that Salvation Army-style ministries were common among evangelical denominations. A common denominator among these activistic evangelical groups is a commitment to some variant of religious perfectionism. This point is made in Timothy L. Smith's *Revivalism and Social Reform* (New York: Abingdon Press, 1957). Perfectionism lurks beneath the surface in Donald W. Dayton's *Discovering an Evangelical Heritage* (New York: Harper & Row Publishers, 1976). A work that ignores perfectionism as a theme, but which deals almost exclusively with perfectionist groups is Norris Magnuson's *Salvation in the Slums: Evangelical Social Work, 1865–1920* (Metuchen, NJ: Scarecrow Press, 1977). My own work is heavily influenced by the paradigmatic constructions of Dayton.

ous, although largely unrecognized, tradition of social reflection and political engagement.[2]

The marginalization of Free Methodist social witness is a result of several factors. The Church's cultural conservatism in matters of dress and entertainment, although historically consistent with its understanding of Methodism, naturally hindered its interaction with North American society. Likewise, the tendency of Free Methodists to funnel their political action through the Prohibition Party contributed to the apparent political and social irrelevancy of the Church.[3]

The Free Methodist Church, like so many of the new religious movements which emerged during the antebellum period, was a product of the religious agitation in the so-called "burned-over district" of western New York. The immediate cause of the organization of the new denomination was the expulsion of B. T. Roberts from the Genesee Conference of the Methodist Episcopal Church in 1858. Roberts had managed to alienate himself from the conference hierarchy through his leadership of the so-called "Nazarite" faction in the Genesee Conference. As products of burned-over district radicalism, Nazarites opposed slavery, secret societies, and perceived doctrinal innovations within Methodism. Especially troubling to Nazarites were several modifications in the Discipline of the Methodist Episcopal Church which appeared during the 1850s.[4] In 1852, the Church's General Conference changed

[2]Among the most important Free Methodist figures engaged in social reflection and political action have been the denomination's founder, B. T. Roberts; Mary Alice Tenney, long-time professor of English at Greenville College; Marston; S. Rickey Kamm, professor of history at Seattle Pacific College and Wheaton College; George A. Turner, professor emeritus, Asbury Theological Seminary; Howard A. Snyder, professor at United Theological Seminary; and David L. McKenna, president of Asbury Theological Seminary. The Free Methodist Church has had two presidential candidates running as members of the Prohibition Party—C. Hoyt Watson (1948) and E. Harold Munn (1960s).

[3]In many ways, the misinterpretation of evangelical ethical formulations is paralleled by misinterpretations of the Prohibition Party. The party's wide range of reform interests has received documentation in Roger C. Storm, *Partisan Prophets: History of the Prohibition Party* (Denver: National Prohibition Foundation, 1972).

[4]On the burned-over district, see Whitney R. Cross, *The Burned-Over District: A Social and Intellectual History of Enthusiastic Religion in Western New York, 1800–1850* (New York: Harper & Row Publishers, 1965). The standard history of the Free Methodist Church is Leslie Ray Marston's *From Age to Age A Living Witness: A Historical Interpretation of Free Methodism's First Century* (Winona Lake, IN: Light and Life Press, 1960).

Methodism's longstanding rule that its churches be built "plain and with free seats" by adding the words "wherever practicable," while the Church's 1856 General Conference removed the Discipline's law forbidding the reception of new members until they laid off "superfluous ornaments."[5] Such modifications in the Discipline of the Methodist Episcopal Church explain, in part, the Nazarite contention that Methodism was abandoning one of the central concerns of John Wesley, namely, the centrality of the mission to the poor in the life of the Church.

Although scholars continue to debate whether Wesley's ministry was beneficial to the poor, especially the British working class, Free Methodists have consistently viewed Wesley's ministry among the poor as defining their own ministry and as being relevant for the reconstruction of society. The recent conclusions of Theodore W. Jennings that Wesley taught that the benefit to the poor should serve as the criterion for judging the ministry of the Church and the state varies little from conclusions drawn by a series of Free Methodist writers since 1860. Not surprisingly, the Nazarites proposed simple economic explanations for the modifications of Church discipline—Methodism had grown "strong" and "wealthy."[6]

Although the issue of pew rental was to play a substantial role in the history of the Free Methodist Church, the actual event that

---

[5]*Earnest Christian,* November 1860, 360. An early Free Methodist interpretation of the declension of Methodism is found in Elias Bowen, *History of the Origin of the Free Methodist Church* (Rochester, NY: B. T. Roberts, 1871).

[6]Theodore W. Jennings, Jr. *Good News to the Poor: John Wesley's Evangelical Economics* (Nashville: Abingdon Press, 1990) 69. Jennings provides material on the academic controversies surrounding Methodism's place in English society. On the same issues, see Theodore Runyon, ed. *Sanctification and Liberation: Liberation Theologies in the Light of the Wesleyan Tradition* (Nashville: Abingdon Press, 1981). Especially noteworthy among Free Methodist works that urge Christians to follow social and economic paradigms established by Wesley is Mary Alice Tenney's *Blueprint for a Christian World: An Analysis of the Wesleyan Way* (Winona Lake, IN: Light and Life Press, 1953). Tenney also circulated her ideas in a condensed version designed for lay people, *Living in Two Worlds: How A Christian Does It!* (Winona Lake, IN: Light and Life Press, 1959). Similar themes are expressed in Marston's *Age to Age A Living Witness,* in the writings of George A. Turner, and in Howard A. Snyder, *The Radical Wesley* (Downers Grove, IL: Inter-Varsity Press, 1979). Wesleyan Church scholar Leon O. Hynson has produced *To Reform the Nation: Foundations of Wesley's Ethics* (Grand Rapids, MI: Francis Asbury Press, 1984). During the 1940s and 1950s, Free Methodists circulated the writings of John W. Bready, an English champion of the social relevance of Wesley. On the modification of Methodist discipline, see Bowen, 245–47.

precipitated Roberts' expulsion from the Genesee Conference was the dissemination of an article written by Roberts entitled "New School Methodism." In it Roberts decried what he perceived to be doctrinal and ethical compromises within the Genesee Conference. The failure of the General Conference of the Methodist Episcopal Church, which met in 1860, to consider Roberts' appeal led to the formation of the Free Methodist Church the same year.

Free Methodist teaching concerning "the preferential option for the poor" cannot be understood apart from the Church's geographical spread and social location. The Church experienced steady, if unspectacular, growth during the nineteenth century. In 1890 Church membership stood at 22,000. By 1916 it had grown to 35,000. For an intensely evangelistic denomination, closely linked to the burgeoning Holiness revival of the nineteenth century, such figures appear modest. A close review of the geographical distribution of Free Methodist membership provides at least a partial explanation for the Church's modest growth. From its inception, Free Methodism remained tied to the areas of New England migration. In 1890, two-thirds of all Free Methodists resided in the Yankee dominated areas of New York, the western reserve of Ohio, Michigan, Illinois, Kansas, and southern Wisconsin. The Yankee preponderance in the Church becomes even more pronounced if one includes Free Methodist membership from other areas with significant numbers of Yankee migrants such as western Pennsylvania, northern Indiana, Iowa, and Minnesota. Such figures, of course, do not tell the entire story. Free Methodists played a significant role in the growth of the Holiness Movement in areas as diverse as South Carolina, Texas, Oklahoma, and the Pacific Northwest. In the South, in particular, the Free Methodist Church's rigid adherence to the cultural mores of its heritage in the burned-over district undermined evangelistic outreach. In such areas, the Church's strict requirements concerning dress, Sabbath observance, and opposition to racially segregated worship were hardly conducive to rapid denominational growth. As the Texas Annual Conference reported in 1912, ". . . our enemies outside the church and some of our own people frequently assert that Free Methodism is a northern institution." When early Free Methodists referred to themselves as "pilgrims," they were not only making allusions to John Bunyan's *Pilgrim's Progress,* they were talking about their biological roots in Puritan New England.[7]

From its inception in 1860, the Free Methodist Church understood its mission as two-fold, "to maintain the Bible standard of Christianity and to preach the gospel to the poor." As a Methodist Episcopal pastor, B. T. Roberts was troubled by the Church's lack of concern for the poor. The very name of the Church, "Free Methodist," signified his determination to found a Church without aristocratic class distinctions. Rental of pews and other "modern" financial expedients for promoting and financing the Church such as festivals, lotteries, fairs, and donation parties were prohibited largely because they catered to the tastes of middle class and wealthy parishioners with discretionary incomes while those without such incomes inevitably would feel excluded from the life of the Church.[8]

The extent to which the Free Methodist Church actually became a Church of the poor is difficult to determine. The common assumption of most students of American religious history that the Holiness Movement, of which the Free Methodist Church is a part, represents a religion of the economically dispossessed, has been based at best on impressionistic evidence. An actual empirical study conducted by Peter Oblinger concluded that Holiness Movement-related-Methodists in Illinois were slightly poorer than non-Holiness Methodists.[9] In 1903, the California Conference of the Free Methodist Church, in a statement on the Church's relationship to labor, observed "our church is made up for the most part of laboring people."[10] A common sense reading of the evidence suggests that Free Methodists were generally lower-middle-class property owners, although poor people did make up a sizeable part of the total Church membership. Among the poor within the Free

[7]*Annual Meetings: Proceedings of the Annual Conferences of the Free Methodist Church,* 1912, 344. On Yankee migration, see Lois Kimball Mathews, *The Expansion of New England: The Spread of New England Settlement and Institutions to the Mississippi River, 1620–1865* (Boston: Houghton Mifflin, 1909). On Free Methodist membership statistics, see H. K. Carroll, *The Religious Forces of the United States* (New York: The Christian Literature Company, 1893) 267–69 and Bureau of the Census, *Religious Bodies,* 1916, 2 vols. (Washington: Government Printing Office, 1919).

[8]*Earnest Christian,* January 1860, 15.

[9]Carl D. Oblinger, *Religious Mimesis: Social Bases for the Holiness Schism in Late Nineteenth Century Methodism* (Evanston, IL: Institute for the Study of American Religion, 1973).

[10]*Annual Minutes,* 1903, 32.

Methodist congregations, one could frequently include the pastor. The 1906 religious census indicated that Free Methodist pastors, with an annual salary of $370 were, along with Wesleyan Methodist pastors, Salvation Army officers, and the pastors of a number of predominately African American Churches, the lowest paid clergy in America.[11] The Church's own statistics for 1915 indicate that the intervening decade had not substantially improved the financial lot of Free Methodist clergy.[12]

Regardless of the actual financial standing of most of its members, Free Methodism remained suspicious of concentrated wealth well into the twentieth century. "Capitalism . . . having secured its hold on nearly all the great industries of the land," the Ohio Annual Conference reported in 1916, "dictates the price of food, clothing and material for shelter and warmth. It forces labor to desecrate the Sabbath. . . . It has cheated poor nations out of their wealth and when they would defend themselves it calls loudly for the dogs of war to advance its interests."[13] Given such a view, it is hardly surprising that Free Methodist pastor Charles M. Damon looked forward in anticipation to a new social order "possible under some form of Christian socialism." In this millennial state, the "sweat system" oppressing labor would be abolished. Women would be "elevated, educated and enfranchised," while African Americans, Indians, and Chinese would no longer be subjected to white racial prejudice.[14]

These early twentieth-century Free Methodist critiques of capitalism are grounded in B. T. Roberts' own insistence that the very practice of pew rental that he so detested was rooted in the burgeoning capitalism of antebellum American society. "The world is not only growing old," Roberts wrote in 1865,

> it is growing rich. . . . In this country many are rich and many more are striving to be. For the salvation of these prosperous classes, the efforts of the religious denominations are generally directed. Church edifices are built as expensively as the means and credit at command will allow. . . . Pecuniary considerations control the

[11]Bureau of the Census, *Religious Bodies,* 1906, vol. 1 (Washington: Government Printing Office, 1910) 96.

[12]*Free Methodist,* 18 January 1916.

[13]*Annual Minutes,* 1916, 322.

[14]Charles M. Damon, *Sketches and Incidents, or Reminiscences of Interest in the Life of the Author* (Chicago: Free Methodist Publishing House, 1900) 249, 307–8.

right to occupancy of a seat. Money commands the pews, and the
pews too often control the pulpit.[15]

As early as 1861, Roberts argued that "it required the close-fisted
selfish spirit of a commercial age, under the influence of the ac-
cumulated corruptions of sixteen centuries, to introduce the cus-
tom of selling seats in the house of God."[16]

Roberts referred to churches that rented pews as "stock
churches." He wrote,

> Men [*sic*] take stock in them as they do in a bank or a railroad; they
> dedicate the house of God, and then sell the right to worship him
> there to the highest bidder! Many a church edifice can be found
> into which a poor person scarcely ventures to enter. . . . Were
> Christ and the apostles to appear as of old, they could hardly find
> a welcome in many aristocratic churches—for they were classed
> among the poor. Never, until of late, were men so 'covetous' that
> they made the right to hear the gospel an article of traffic.[17]

"A system that looks at finding a good market, at a high price for
pews," Roberts wrote in 1872, "is not of Christ. It has no warrant in the gospel. It cannot summon a single precept of the New
Testament to its support. . . . To the banquet Jesus has provided
all are invited to come and eat without money and without price."[18]

The increase of wealth and conspicuous consumption engen-
dered by the American Civil War was deeply troubling to Roberts.
He was particularly critical of those who argued that churches
needed to be made more attractive "to refine public taste" and
to maintain the loyalty of the wealthy members. As Roberts criti-
cally observed, "Suppose the rich do leave you. They left the savior when he was on earth." In fact, Roberts maintained that
elaborate and expensive churches required a rich clientele. The crisis confronting Methodism, Roberts insisted, was rooted in American Christianity's subservience to wealth. This crisis, Roberts
argued, could have been averted had Methodism remained faithful to its understanding of the corrupting influence of wealth. As
Roberts quoted from the discarded disciplines of the Methodist
Episcopal Church, "the corrupting influence of wealth is not con-

[15]*Earnest Christian,* February 1865, 60.
[16]Ibid., January 1861, 17–18.
[17]Ibid., March 1863, 72.
[18]Ibid., June 1872, 190.

fined to the Methodist Church, but extends to all denominations. When any church cannot get along without rich men farewell to gospel purity."[19]

Roberts consistently warned his followers that prosperity posed the supreme test of religious commitment. "There is no class of society," Roberts warned in 1870, "in such imminent danger of eternal damnation as the rich. If any of them are saved, it will be like Lot coming out of Sodom—the exception, and not the rule."[20] Contradicting the prosperity theology common to Gilded Age America, Roberts asserted that Jesus forbids his disciples to accumulate wealth. As Roberts wrote in 1865,

. . . the master in plain words forbids his disciples to amass wealth, to lay it up—not in the heart, for thieves cannot break into that, but on earth, in any form, in any place beneath the skies. He forbids them from storing up money which they will not want—from adding farm to farm, and house to house, and bond to bond, and store to store, and ship to ship. Anything that passes for treasure among men [*sic*] of the world, we are forbidden to lay up. What can be plainer? Yet do not the mass of professing Christians act as though Jesus, instead of forbidding it, had commanded us to lay up treasures on earth?[21]

Drawing primarily from Lukan texts, Roberts observed that in the New Testament only two rich men became disciples of Jesus— Zaccheus and Joseph of Arimathea. Roberts suggested to his readers that, in both cases, if they remained faithful to the gospel, they relinquished their wealth. "For we read that when the spirit was poured out upon the disciples upon the day of Pentecost," Roberts wrote, "all that believed were together, and had all things in common, and sold their possessions and goods, and imparted to all, as every man [*sic*] had need. This is the way rich men took to get saved in the days when conditions of salvation were clearly understood."[22]

Roberts did believe that a few rich people might possibly be saved if they met the approved gospel conditions. But Roberts insisted they must meet two conditions, restitution where wrong has oc-

[19]Ibid., March 1867, 158–59.
[20]Ibid., January 1870, 30–31.
[21]Ibid., February 1865, 60–62; see also *Earnest Christian*, January 1870, 30–31; April 1876, 134–35; and June 1864, 188.
[22]Ibid., February 1865, 60.

curred such as the defrauding of workers, and the entire consecration of one's property to God. "If, in his providence, he [God] places property at your disposal, you can retain for your own use no more than will furnish an income sufficient to enable you, and those dependent upon you, to live in a comfortable, plain, Christian manner." Roberts did not reject capitalism as an economic system. "If God gives you ability to get wealth," he wrote, "use it—not for self-aggrandizement but for the good of your race."[23]

Unlike the rich who followed Christ only rarely, "the poor, as a class," Roberts observed, "heard him [Jesus] gladly." The gospel, Roberts insisted, would inevitably expose the pride of the rich, the refined, and the educated, for "there was a portion of divine truth which wealthy members, as a class, would not receive." But Roberts noted that "in the poor, pride, the mother of all sin, has not been so strongly developed, not so deeply rooted. . . . They are not so prone to feel that they can themselves prescribe the terms on which they will become Christians. They are more willing to endure hardships as good soldiers of Jesus."[24]

The poor were not only more receptive to the gospel. It was this class which produced the most productive Christians. People notorious for their sins, such as John Bunyan, an illiterate profane tinker, under the power of the gospel "may result in greater good to the cause of God, than uniting with the church of kings, nobles, of senators and judges. Constantine," Roberts concluded, "embracing Christianity injured it more than all his predecessors had done by their persecutions." Yet Roberts observed that the entire American religious enterprise was committed to placating the wealthy in their sins.[25]

For Roberts and other Free Methodists, the single most pressing reason for making the mission to the poor the central mission of the Church was its hermeneutical role in the teaching of the Lukan Jesus. As Roberts noted, when John the Baptist inquired if Jesus were the Messiah, the savior answered that the blind see, the lame walk, the deaf hear, the dead are raised, and the poor have the gospel preached to them. In effect, Jesus' ministry among the poor was a miracle on a par with cleansing lepers and raising the

[23]Ibid., 62–63.
[24]Ibid., March 1864, 71.
[25]Ibid., 70–71.

dead. As Roberts argued, this was the gospel's greatest miracle, greater than raising the dead, because it broke down barriers that separate economic and social classes. As he wrote, "those who see the gospel eradicating pride from the hearts of men, and blending all classes in one holy, loving brotherhood, need no argument to prove it divine; . . . while all argument is lost upon those who see in it only a system of religious aristocracy, catering to fostering a spirit of pride and exclusiveness." It was for this reason Free Methodists argued that partiality be given the poor in the preaching of the gospel.[26]

Early Free Methodists would have agreed with Gustavo Gutiérrez and liberation theology in rejecting the sentimentalism so common in the ministries among the poor. Liberation theologians' assertions that one must be in solidarity with the poor, living among the poor, and sharing the suffering of the poor have parallels in Roberts's writings. "A Christian," Roberts wrote, "goes among the poor—not with the condescending air of a patron—but with the feeling of a brother. . . . In the Christian congregation the rich and poor meet together on terms of equality, and no preference is given to a man on account of his riches, or his gay and costly apparel."[27]

Like liberation theologian Gutiérrez, Roberts and the movement he led were suspicious of those who emphasized orthodox creedal affirmation while making behavioral norms matters of secondary importance. It is this concern with orthopraxy, or orthodox practice, which characterizes much of liberation theology's critique of establishment Christianity. As Gutiérrez has written, "Jesus calls himself the truth, but also describes himself as the way and the life (see John 14:6). His actions and words, his practice, show us the course to follow. The Lord proclaims a truth that must be put into practice; that is why works are regarded as so important throughout the New Testament."[28] The same concerns are evident in Roberts's insistence that the Biblical doctrine of "union with Christ" was not only salvific but also ethically binding. He argued that no belief in a creed nor adherence to forms could make one

[26]Ibid., 70.
[27]Ibid., March 1871, 160.
[28]Gustavo Gutiérrez, *A Theology of Liberation: History, Politics and Salvation*, Sister Caridad Inda and John Eagleson, trans. and ed. (Maryknoll, NY: Orbis Books, 1973) 301–2.

a follower of Jesus. Instead, a Christian is one who obeys Jesus' teachings and shares his sympathies. "The spirit of Christ," Roberts maintained, "was one of sympathy with the poor. His associates were from that class. He gave it the crowning proof of his messiahship that the poor have the gospel preached to them. A Christian feels this way. He goes among the poor."[29]

Another example of Roberts's use of orthopraxy to define traditional theological concepts was his use of the imagery of *kenosis,* or Christ's condescension in becoming a human being, as described in 2 Corinthians 8:9. Christ, Roberts held, was emptied not merely of his divine status, but of material wealth as well. Further, the purpose of Paul's teaching, for Roberts, was not to create a new theological concept but to encourage Christian benevolence. Jesus was not merely one's savior. He was to be treated as ethically normative.[30]

The centrality of the lifestyle aspects of religious practice in the lives of Free Methodists has frequently been dismissed, even by Free Methodists, as a manifestation of fanatical legalism. However, such social conservatism bears a striking resemblance to the counsel at the Medellín Conference that priests "give testimony of poverty and detachment from material goods."[31] This counsel would appear to have grown out of a sensitivity similar to that which led Free Methodists to oppose wedding rings, ties, feathers in bonnets, and colorful dresses. Free Methodist standards of dress and behavior were considered extreme, or radical, even among socially conservative evangelicals. During the nineteenth century, Free Methodists especially gloried in being labeled radicals. "The Bible is a radical book," Roberts wrote in one of his most widely circulated editorials. "It never proposes half-way measures. The word radical comes from *radix*—root—and the Bible always goes to the root of the matter. Look at its treatment of sin. It never tolerates it for a moment. . . . To serve God moderately," Roberts concluded, "is to serve the devil fully."[32]

[29]*Earnest Christian,* March 1871, 160.
[30]Ibid.
[31]On the Medellín Conference, see Second General Conference of Latin American Bishops, *The Church in the Present-Day Transformation of Latin America in the Light of the Council,* vol. 2: *Conclusions,* 2nd ed. (Washington, DC: Division for Latin America-United States Catholic Conference, 1973) 193.
[32]*Earnest Christian,* February 1869, 37–39.

Free Methodists viewed their social conservatism, or radicalism, as an intimate part of their denomination's social witness. In fact, the most notable feature of Free Methodist social teaching was the Church's refusal to accept as legitimate the dualism that existed between personal behavior and public policy in many Protestant ethical formulations. A survey of Free Methodist Annual Conference reports reveals a Church equally concerned with the evils of intemperance, ostentatious dress, economic monopoly, and racial injustice. This is hardly surprising. As a Church deeply involved in the lives of the poor, but with limited access to the seats of power, Free Methodists tended to focus less on systemic solutions to the economic problems faced by the poor than on lifestyle changes that the poor could initiate themselves. This meant, for example, that Free Methodists, including Roberts, viewed prohibition of the sale of liquor not as a private concern, but as a measure that would greatly improve the lives of poor people. As Free Methodist reformer Olin M. Owen wrote in 1892, "We have protection for monopolies and salonists in short, protection for the rich, but where is the protection for the poor?"[33] Similarly, the Church saw its rules against "putting on gold or costly apparel," not as purely personal matters but as having profound social and economic relevance to the poor. "Domineering, dogmatic, extravagant and senseless fashion," the Ohio Annual Conference steamed in 1916, "outraging beauty, improvising the pocket book, inviting lust, destroying health and wasting time . . . God's judgment endorses following the settled and useful customs of dress for the sake of economy and convenience."[34]

Closely involved in the lives of the poor, Roberts and other Free Methodists saw the poor not as an abstract social class but as actual human beings whose fate rested, at least partially, in the Church's own actions. Therefore, direct action to meet immediate human needs was not optional. It was, in fact, mandatory.[35]

[33]Olin M. Owen, *Rum, Rags, and Religion, or In Darkest America and the Way Out* (Buffalo: A. W. Hall, 1896) 35.

[34]*Annual Minutes,* 1916, 322.

[35]The Holiness Movement Church, which merged with the Free Methodist Church in 1959, even codified the Church's responsibility to the poor in its discipline, observing "that they [members of the Holiness Movement Church] allow none to suffer hunger in the community in which they live." This same Church's rigorous proscription against extravagance in dress was rooted in similar concern

Roberts, and the Free Methodist Church, taught that the transformation of lifestyle, in conformity with their Church's understanding of the word of God, was the first step toward the empowerment of the poor and the marginalized. Given such views, even the most innocent violation of the Church's detailed code of personal behavior could be viewed as an alarming expression of antinomianism. As a result, the private acts of Free Methodists were laden with social meaning. For example, the church which used "oyster suppers," a popular form of entertainment for young people in the upper-middle-class Methodist churches, to raise funds, or simply as social entertainment, was making a statement about the focus of its ministry. It was, in effect, separating itself from its prime vocation of serving those unable to buy admittance, the poor. It was in the process of separating itself from Jesus who had come to level all class distinctions.

Closely related to the theme of the "preferential option for the poor" in the writings of B. T. Roberts are Roberts' views concerning race and gender and his fairly extensive writings on agriculture and the monetary system. On race, Roberts was deeply committed to the abolition of slavery and the granting of full civil rights to African Americans. He was particularly proud of the fact that the first Free Methodist Church organized in St. Louis, Missouri, was interracial and banned slave owners from Church membership. In later years, Free Methodists, following Roberts, opposed the exclusion of Chinese immigrants from the United States and championed the rights of Japanese-Americans in the West.

Likewise, Roberts strongly supported the burgeoning women's rights movement of the late nineteenth century. He was deeply committed to both women's suffrage and the ordination of women into the ministry. Roberts' views were controversial even in his own Church. At the Church's General Conference he introduced a resolution to permit the ordination of women. In response to its rejection, Roberts wrote his last book, *Ordaining Women*. "The gospel of Jesus Christ," Roberts concluded, "knows no distinction of race,

for the poor. "We should not on any account," the Church noted in its discipline, "spend what the Lord has put into our hands, as stewards to be useful for his glory, on expensive apparel, when thousands are suffering for food and raiment and millions are perishing for the word of life" (*The Doctrine and Discipline of the Holiness Movement, or Church* [Ottawa, ON: Holiness Movement Publishing House, 1907] 21, 30).

condition, or sex; therefore no person evidently called of God to the gospel ministry, and duly qualified for it, should be refused ordination on account of race, condition, or sex."[36]

Roberts' commitment to racial and sexual equality was rivaled by his interest in the plight of farmers during the long period of deflation that followed the Civil War. In an 1872 address at the Monroe County (New York) Fair, Roberts urged that "stringent laws against trusts and combinations" be enacted to protect agriculture.[37] Roberts also supported the organization of non-oathbound farmer societies. He was sympathetic to many of the political goals of the Populist Movement, although Roberts explicitly rejected the secretism of the Southern Alliance which he not inaccurately attributed to Southern racial prejudice.[38]

Roberts was especially critical of the deflationary monetary policies of the post-bellum era. In correspondence with Greenback Party presidential candidate Peter Cooper, Roberts expressed his support for that party's policy of regulated currency expansion through the printing of paper money. For similar reasons, Roberts supported the unlimited coinage of silver. His criticism of national monetary policies resulted in the publication of a book, *First Lessons on Money,* in 1886. In it, Roberts observed that his long association with "common people from New England to California, and from Dakota to Texas" had given him an opportunity "to witness the distress which the bad management of our finances by our national government had produced." Roberts concluded that the country needed an elastic currency and the enactment of laws that "make it difficult to amass vast fortunes" that remain in the hands of an aristocracy of wealth. Roberts also encouraged that "the people . . . see that their representatives in Congress pass laws in their interests, and not in favor of money class and rich corporations." By such advice, Roberts was not advocating the abolition of capitalism or of private property. However, Roberts did believe that concentrated wealth posed a danger to the community, and to the souls of those who possessed it. To safeguard the community, Roberts suggested that money be regulated. As Roberts made abundantly

[36]B. T. Roberts, *Ordaining Women* (Rochester, NY: Earnest Christian Publication Co., 1891) 159.
[37]*Earnest Christian,* November 1872, 163.
[38]*Free Methodist,* 8 April 1891.

clear, religious life could not be separated from economic and social analysis. It was the task of the Church to speak for those being dispossessed by mammon.[39]

For a small Church, the actual extent of direct Free Methodist involvement in the lives of the poor was quite impressive. Even though Free Methodism remained a predominately rural denomination well into the twentieth century, the Church operated a string of urban rescue missions in cities such as New York, Pittsburgh, Kansas City, Omaha, Wichita, Oklahoma City, Chicago, and Atlanta. Although these missions placed great emphasis upon spiritual salvation, their very location among the poor forced them frequently to serve as advocates. Not atypical was the career of Jane Dunning, a Free Methodist laywoman from Binghamton, New York, who operated a rescue mission among African Americans in New York City during the 1860s and 1870s. Dunning and her associates fed, bathed, and attempted to solve the immediate everyday problems of people living in poverty. Dunning's ministry was duplicated in many settings. For example, Chicago's Olive Branch Mission continues to feed and shelter the homeless as Chicago's oldest rescue mission. Like the Salvation Army, Free Methodists established a network of homes for unwed mothers while vigorously attacking the double standard in sexual ethics which virtually forced unmarried women into prostitution while treating male promiscuity as a mere misdemeanor. Earlier Free Methodist women had served as teachers among freed slaves in the South following the Civil War. Other Free Methodists served in missions sponsored by other denominations. It was not uncommon for even small Free Methodist congregations to sponsor rescue missions or homes for unwed mothers, hold street meetings, or, at least, circulate religious literature among the poor.

Although early Free Methodism contained much to recommend it to those concerned about living the gospel, Free Methodist interpretations cannot be viewed as having been normative or faultless. In fact, Free Methodist interpretations were rooted in a particular North American milieu that was culturally tied to the Church's heritage as a Yankee immigrant phenomenon. As such, its limitations are readily identifiable. Free Methodists were cap-

---

[39]Quoted in Clarence Howard Zahniser, *Earnest Christian: Life of Benjamin Titus Roberts* (Rochester, NY: by the author, 1957) 283–84.

able of legalism, rank anti-Catholicism, and cultural triumphalism—faults which were certainly not the unique property of Free Methodists and which can readily be seen in many constituent groups within North American evangelicalism. Critics of evangelicalism have frequently used these faults to suggest that evangelicals have little to contribute to ecumenical ethical discourse. However, Free Methodists and other similar evangelical groups must be recognized for their roles in the maintenance of the idea of the "preferential option for the poor" as a common thread throughout the history of Christianity—a thread which may wax and wane among particular groups, but one which is constantly picked up by others to pass to succeeding generations. Increased historical awareness of these religious traditions and groups, including the Free Methodist Church, can contribute to the identifying and transcending of the barriers that separate Christians.

Chapter Four

Comunidades Eclesiales de Base and Autonomous Local Churches: Catholic Liberationists meet Baptist Landmarkers

Bill J. Leonard

"Even the church of Rome is a local Church."

Henrique Vaz, Liberation Theologian

"A scriptural church is a local congregation . . ."

J. M. Pendleton, Old Landmarker

When Anthony Dunnavant asked me to consider participating in this project I was skeptical. I was uncertain that one could or should read elements of nineteenth-century evangelical theology into twentieth-century liberation theology or vice versa. Yet as I studied various documents related to liberation theology, particularly those written by Leonardo Boff, the Brazilian Franciscan, I was struck by liberationist descriptions of local churches, ecclesial freedom and democratic polity.* Many of these themes sounded strangely similar to those found in the writings of various nineteenth-century evangelicals, specifically those Baptists known as Old Landmarkers. Clearly, the two movements are divided by irreconcilable differences of time, place and, most importantly, theology. Yet reading liberation theology with an eye to Old Landmarkism helped me hear and reflect on both movements in new ways. For example, a study of liberation theology and Old Landmarkism requires us to reexamine the continuing tension between

---

*Editor's Note: As this book goes to press, Leonardo Boff's resignation from the priesthood was recently announced.

the Church as particular congregation and the Church as universal communion. It forces us to ask once again: How does political idealism affect theological speculation? What is the role of persecution and oppression in shaping one's view of the nature of the Church and the nature of theology? How does one's reading of Holy Scripture from a minority or an establishment perspective influence that person's understanding of Church, theology, and Scripture itself?

Liberation theology is a complex ideology and a movement given to great diversity of thought and practice. In this brief article it is impossible to trace the multitude of themes and theories which have characterized the movement since its inception mid-century. Rather, this study represents an attempt to understand liberation theology in light of certain parallels it may or may not have with aspects of nineteenth-century North American Protestantism, specifically the theology of those Baptists known as Old Landmarkers. This is not to suggest that these Protestants were complete prototypes of liberation theologians, far from it. Yet to read them in light of liberation theology is to gain a new sense of their radicality within their own particular historical and cultural context. Likewise, Old Landmark theories regarding the nature of the Church, particularly the local congregation, may help us understand liberationist views on base ecclesial communities *(comunidades eclesiales de base)* in a new way. This is especially evident in relation to the individual Christian community or congregation. An important description of the nature of the Church in its grassroots expression—growing up from the people rather than down through the hierarchy—is found in the activities of so-called base ecclesial communities as described by Leonardo Boff in such works as *Church, Charism, and Power.* In similar or at least parallel ways, Landmark writers such as J. R. Graves and J. M. Pendleton sought to establish a form of New Testament primitivism as the foundation for their version of base ecclesial communities: the local congregation of baptized Christian believers. They believed that the true faith had been kept alive since the first century in a succession of faithful but oppressed congregations. As they saw it, Baptist Churches alone possessed the marks of the true Church passed on across the centuries through a persecuted minority of Christian believers. From the Landmark perspective, the local congregation was the primary ecclesial expression of the Church's authority and identity.

On reading liberation theology alongside certain documents relative to nineteenth-century Protestantism one is immediately struck by two important and parallel themes: the Christocentric nature of human spiritual and political liberation; and the concern to free persons from the control of governmental and ecclesiastical establishments. In his now classic work, *A Theology of Liberation*, Gustavo Gutiérrez writes:

> In the Bible, Christ is presented as the one who brings us liberation. Christ the savior liberates man [*sic*] from sin, which is the ultimate root of all disruption of friendship and of all injustice and oppression. Christ makes man [*sic*] truly free . . . he enables man [*sic*] to live in communion with him, and this is the basis for all human brotherhood.[1]

Christ is the foundation of liberation for the individual and the society.

Gutiérrez leads the way in criticizing "those dominant groups who have always used the Church to defend their interests and maintain their privileged position. . . ."[2] He concludes that:

> The denunciation of injustice implies the rejection of the use of Christianity to legitimize the established order. It likewise implies that the church has entered into conflict with those who wield power. And finally it leads to acknowledging the need for the separation of Church and state because "this is of primary importance in liberating the Church from the temporal ties and from the image projected by its bonds with the powerful."[3]

In *A Theology of Liberation*, Gutiérrez traces the rise of the established Church—its growing concern for its own power, its relationship with the political powers and interests, and its exclusivist dogmas. He calls the Church to return to the model of the "first centuries" (his own form of primitivism) in its ability to respond spontaneously to the needs of the world.[4]

In his reflection on and analysis of the documents and spirit of the Medellín conference (1968), Gutiérrez cites various liberationist

[1]Gustavo Gutiérrez, *A Theology of Liberation: History, Politics, and Salvation*, Sister Caridad Inda and John Eagleson, trans. and ed. (Maryknoll, NY: Orbis Books, 1973) 37.
[2]Ibid., 65.
[3]Ibid., 115, citing *Iglesia Latinoamericana*, 314–15.
[4]Ibid., 256–57.

issues which might well have received a sympathetic response from many nineteenth-century Protestants, even Landmarkers. Indeed, they would be shocked to hear a Roman Catholic articulating these views. Such concepts include: 1) The "prophetic denunciation of grave injustices rampant in Latin America."[5] This has clear implications for issues of separation of Church and state and religious freedom. 2) The need for "conscienticizing evangelization." The God known in the Bible is the liberating God. 3) The Church's identification with the poor. This means discovering a Church of the poor which rejects power and materialism. 4) The Church must be Christocentric. He writes: "The Church cannot be a prophet in our day if she herself is not turned to Christ."[6] 5) A renewal of the clergy in spirit and lifestyle. Gutiérrez agrees that "a secular job could be very healthy," in the clergy's ability to live without dependence on the establishment and identify more completely with the people.[7] His understanding of the Church leads him to call upon the clergy to establish closer identification with the people, a twentieth-century "farmer-preacher," perhaps.

Gutiérrez's seminal work must be considered alongside the insights of Leonardo Boff regarding the changing nature of the Church in Latin America. Boff and other liberation theologians articulate a controversial theology relative to "base church (or ecclesial) communities," which have developed in response to the needs of grassroots Christians in Latin America. Alfred T. Hennelly suggests that the formation of basic ecclesial communities was one of "three key components of liberation theology's initial phase," as early as the 1950s.[8] He describes these communities as small groups of Catholics gathered together for prayer, worship, and communal response to spiritual and secular issues which affect them. Often organized or guided by lay leaders, the groups also provide for mutual encouragement, Bible study, dialogue, and genuine community outside the often anonymous formal structures of the established Church.[9]

[5]Ibid., 114.
[6]Ibid., 118.
[7]Ibid.
[8]Alfred T. Hennelly, ed., *Liberation Theology: A Documentary History* (Maryknoll, NY: Orbis Books, 1990) xxvi.
[9]Ibid.

Students of liberation theology are divided as to the relationship between base ecclesial communities and liberationist ideology. Some suggest that base communities are the vehicle for implementing liberation theology, while others believe that "liberation theology emerges from the experience and reflection of the base communities."[10] Hennelly finds a synthesis, not a contradiction, in these two analyses which reflects the mutual interaction of both base communities and liberation theology.

Leonardo Boff notes that these communities "sprang up" in reaction to the "heavily hierarchical framework" of existing Church structures. Such hierarchy, he believes, produced "mechanical, reified inequality and inequities" in the Church.[11] He contends that these new communities began as the people "themselves took responsibility for their destiny." This generally "originated with reading the Bible and proceeded to the creation of small basic ecclesial communities (comunidades eclesiales de base)."[12] Uriel Molina Oliu agrees, contending that, "The Bible provided us with the basic impulse which pushed us into the struggle for the transformation of the existing state of affairs."[13] Oliu insists that this is nothing surprising since the poor have a "sixth sense which enables them to grasp the message of the Bible."[14]

These popular-based cell-groups have many names, including basic ecclesial (or Christian) communities, the popular church (Igreja Popular), People's Christian Community (Comunidad Cristiana Popular), or the church born of the people (Igreja que nasce do povo). Boff suggests that basic ecclesial communities, "represent a new experience of the church." They "deserve to be contemplated, welcomed and respected as salvific events."[15] Boff himself describes base communities as composed of small groups of Christians gathered in particular locations for prayer, study of the Scrip-

---

[10]Ibid., xix.

[11]Leonardo Boff, *Ecclesiogenesis: The Base Communities Reinvent the Church*, Robert R. Barr, trans. (Maryknoll, NY: Orbis Books, 1986) 1.

[12]Leonardo Boff, *Church, Charism, and Power: Liberation Theology and the Institutional Church*, John W. Dierchsmeier, trans. (New York: Crossroad, 1984) 8.

[13]Uriel Molina Oliu, "How a People's Christian Community (*Comunidad Cristiana Popular*) is Structured and How it Functions," in *The People of God Amidst the Poor*, Leonardo Boff and Virgil Elizondo, eds., (Edinburgh: T. & T. Clark Ltd, 1984) 5.

[14]Ibid.

[15]Leonardo Boff, *Ecclesiogenesis*, 1.

tures, spiritual encouragement, and varying types of political response. They are often founded or guided by clergy but are built on a high degree of lay participation and cooperation. They developed outside or alongside existing Church structures, and are what some might call ecclesiolae in ecclesia, little churches within the Church. Proponents suggest that these new forms of the Church grew out of a very practical crisis: the shortage of ministers which created new opportunities for the laity. Boff concludes that in base communities, "we are not dealing with the expansion of an existing ecclesiastical system, rotating on a sacramental, clerical axis, but with another form of being church, rotating on the axis of the word and the laity."[16] Thus, base communities are themselves creating "a new ecclesiology, formulating new concepts of theology."[17] Boff notes that while the movement is just developing, it may well represent "a new institutional type of church."[18] The very existence of these grass-roots churches raises significant questions regarding the nature of the Church, the roles of clergy and laity, and the relationship between peoples' churches and the institutional Church. Many of these questions were evident within nineteenth-century American Protestantism. As noted earlier, this study examines certain parallels in those movements within the context of American Christianity and culture. It asks what, if anything, did these movements have in common? How did their cultural and historical setting inform their understanding of the Church itself?

Boff traces the origins of the base church communities to Brazil and the community evangelization efforts in Rio de Janeiro during the early 1960s. These communities were "peoples' movements," born of the needs of the moment and the inadequacies of existing ecclesial structures. He writes that, "Christian life in the basic communities is characterized by the absence of alienating structures, by direct relationships, by reciprocity, by a deep communion, by mutual assistance, by communality of gospel ideals, by equality among members."[19] He notes that these communities developed "in place of a church-society with centralized and hierarchical authority, with autonomous and functional relation-

---

[16]Ibid., 2.
[17]Ibid.
[18]Ibid.
[19]Ibid., 4.

ships. . . ."[20] They were individual, localized communions based
on "participatory relationships."[21] They were truly the Church of
the people.

Boff makes it clear that these basic communities are not separate churches, but reflect the continuing polarity between institution and community in the Latin American milieu. He declares
that, "The church sprung from the people is the same as the church
sprung from the apostles."[22] This statement has at least two implications. First, it means that basic communities are true churches
and that they are not schismatic, sectarian communities. In this
regard, Boff asserts that the New Testament reveals two basic understandings of the Church, both interrelated. "The church is
one;" and "the church is multiple."[23] He cites Henrique Vaz's
statement that, "We have the universal church, which is intrinsi-
cally differentiated, or manifested in the particularity of the local
churches. (Even the church in Rome is local.)"[24] Local faith communities must be taken seriously for themselves as true churches
of Christ.

Boff goes to great lengths to establish the true churchliness of
the particular Christian communities in words which, we shall see,
parallel many statements of nineteenth century Landmark Baptists.
He writes:

> The particular church is the universal church (the salvific will in Christ
> through the Spirit) in its phenomenal, or sacramental, presentation.
> The particular church is the universal church concretized; and in
> being concretized . . . assuming the limits of place, time, culture
> and human beings. The particular church is the whole mystery of
> salvation in Christ—the universal church—in history, but not the
> totality of the history of the mystery of salvation in Christ.[25]

The individual community of faith can be taken seriously for itself, not simply as a part of the entire body of Christ. It contains
in itself elements of the one unique Church.

[20]Leonardo Boff, "A Theological Examination of the Terms 'People of God'
and 'Popular Church,' " in *The People of God Amidst the Poor*, 89-90.
[21]Ibid.
[22]Leonardo Boff, *Ecclesiogenesis*, 7.
[23]Ibid., 16.
[24]Ibid., 17.
[25]Ibid., 19.

For Boff, the particular communities are gathered around common faith in Christ. Indeed, he says, faith in Jesus Christ is the "initiating and structuring principle of the particular church."[26] Through such faith, base communities "are already, in themselves, the presence of the universal church."[27] Shared faith constitutes the basis of unity within and among the whole people of God. Thus Boff unites the concept and practice of basic Christian communities with the centrality of salvation in Jesus Christ, a major theme of liberation theology.

The "Letter to the Peoples of the Third World," written in 1967 by eighteen bishops from churches in ten countries, also reflects this idea. It declares that the gospel begins with conversion "from sin to grace, from egotism to love, from haughtiness to humble service. This conversion is not simply interior and spiritual; it involves the whole man [*sic*] corporeally and socially as well as spiritually and personally. It has a communitarian aspect that is fraught with consequences for society as a whole."[28] Such views mirror those expressed by Gustavo Gutiérrez: "If there is a finality inscribed in history, then the essence of Christian faith is to believe in Christ, that is, to believe that God is irreversibly committed to human history. To believe in Christ, then is to believe that God has made a commitment to the historical development of the human race."[29] Christ is at the center of all human salvation and liberation.

While individual-particular communities participate in the entire Church, they also maintain an identity and authority—dare we suggest an autonomy—of their own. Boff writes that, "No particular church (no diocesan church, Roman or any other, however illustrious its apostolic tradition, its liturgy, and its saints and doctors) may close in upon itself or impose itself upon others and constrain them to accept its particularities."[30] The particular congregation of faithful Christians has an authority in and of itself. These churches are, in the fullest sense, charismatic communities. That is, individuals, whether clergy or laity, share all the charisms

---

[26]Ibid.

[27]Ibid.

[28]"A Letter to the Peoples of the Third World," in *Liberation Theology: A Documentary History*, 49.

[29]Gustavo Gutiérrez, *Toward a Theology of Liberation*, 74.

[30]Leonardo Boff, *Ecclesiogenesis*, 20.

which the Spirit may give. All work together for the building up of the community of faith. Boff calls this the "reinvention of the church."[31] In this process, he believes, "The church is being born at the grassroots, beginning to be born in the heart of God's People."[32]

Boff does not deny the need for and function of an ordained clergy. He does interpret the relationship of clergy and laity in the Church, however. He notes that the specific charism in any Christian believer, "is not outside the community, but within it; not over the community, but for the good of the community."[33] In these diagrams Boff distinguishes between classical ecclesiology and the liberationist model of the People of God.

Classical Ecclesiology:	People of God:
God	
Christ	Christ-Holy Spirit
Apostles	Community-People of God
Bishops	Bishop-Priest-Coordinator
Priests	
Faithful[34]	

In basic communities, laity are full participants in the church's ministry and decision-making. Thus these communities aid "the whole church in the process of declericalization, by restoring to the whole People of God . . . the rights of which they have been deprived. . . ."[35] Indeed, Boff repudiates the idea of the Church as a "hierarchiology—a conception of the church from the top down in dissociation from the People of God. . . ."[36] He insists that, "At the start, everyone in the People of God is equal, a citizen of the kingdom. The mission of the People of God is not entrusted only to a few but is given to all; sacred power is, initially, held by everyone and only later is held by sacred ministers."[37] He concludes that the base ecclesial community is "the place where a true democracy of the people is practiced, where everything is discussed

[31]Ibid., 23.
[32]Ibid.
[33]Ibid., 28.
[34]Leonardo Boff, *Church: Charism and Power*, 133.
[35]Leonardo Boff, *Ecclesiogenesis*, 32.
[36]Ibid., 53.
[37]Leonardo Boff, *Church: Charism and Power*, 155.

and decided together, where critical thought is encouraged."[38] Boff believes that a genuine "ecclesiogenesis" is developing around the world as the Church is "born from the faith of the poor."[39] Many of these concepts sound strangely like those expressed by certain nineteenth-century Protestants as the American nation took shape. They are evident particularly, though not exclusively, among those nineteenth-century Baptists known as Old Landmarkers.

Old Landmarkism is the name for a movement which prevailed among Baptists as early as the 1850s, with particular strength in the American South. It is important to this study for several reasons. First, Landmarkism is a form of successionism—that effort to trace ecclesial authority from Christ and the apostles across history to the contemporary Church. Landmark adherents believed that they stood in an unbroken line of Christian believers dating from Jesus' baptism in the Jordan River by none other than John the Baptist. Unlike Catholic tradition, however, Landmarkism did not base ecclesial authority on apostolic succession through the episcopacy. Rather, Landmarkists traced their lineage through a succession of apostolic Churches, preserved by crypto-baptist communions since the first century. These New Testament Churches were ever outside "establishment" Christianity, that element claiming the name Christian but corrupted from the true gospel since the fourth century when the Constantinian compromise brought the world into the Church. Landmark churches alone bore the true "marks" of the Church and therefore were alone the true churches of Jesus Christ. They possessed the sole authority from Christ to administer sacraments (Landmarkists said ordinances) and receive members into the Body of Christ.

Second, the Landmark understanding of the Church was grounded exclusively in the local congregation. Thus the particular congregation was in itself the true expression of the Church of Jesus Christ. Landmark descriptions of the nature of the local congregation parallel certain views relating to base communities as expressed by Leonardo Boff and other liberation theologians. While there are significant differences, the liberationist reassertion of the importance of particular, grass-roots congregations often sounds

[38]Ibid., 9.
[39]Ibid.

surprisingly like that of the Old Landmark description of the role and authority of the local church.

Third, while many Protestant historians have long viewed Old Landmarkism as displaying an unbending conservativism and obsession with its brand of orthodoxy, the early leaders of the movement—J. R. Graves (1820–1893) and J. M. Pendleton (1811–1891)—demonstrate a strong sense of democratic idealism and a concern for the radical freedom of the gospel. Likewise, they reflect an aggressive opposition to religious and political establishments, both Protestant and Catholic, which may threaten the freedom of conscience and the separation of the state and the Church. This optimism about democratic possibilities coincides with prevailing progressivism evident within much of the nineteenth-century free church tradition. Democracy would overcome establishments and bring freedom to the individual in both Church and society, in the new American nation and throughout the world. America was itself the model and vehicle for the birth of democratic institutions around the globe.

Landmarkism appeared on the American scene at a time of denominational formation and theological fomentation. The nineteenth century witnessed the westward movement of the population and the growth of new denominational configurations. Anti-establishment sentiments prevailed along with competition and theological debate. In the absence of a state Church, religious groups needed "volunteers" who would unite around that one particular vision of the gospel which seemed most biblically sound and spiritually vital. Each sect claimed closest kinship with the primitive New Testament Church in polity, enthusiasm and orthodoxy. Peoples' churches flourished in post-Revolutionary America. Democratic idealism helped soften doctrines of Calvinistic determinism and Divine sovereignty while encouraging free will and direct human participation in the salvific process. Freedom in the Church and the state was a powerful concern to many citizens of the Republic. A genuine sense of liberation permeated the secular and ecclesial environments. In churches old and new the laity reasserted itself in ministering and administering the affairs of the congregation.

Denominations adapted to the frontier setting in ways which would facilitate the spreading of the gospel. Methodist congregations, particularly on the post-Revolutionary frontier, were often lay-centered, tied together through the itinerant ministry of the circuit-riding preacher. They represent one type of nineteenth-century base ecclesial community bringing Christian faith to the new nation. Many churches were organized around a collection of small groups known as the class and the band. The latter was a gathering of persons of same sex for prayer, confession, and encouragement. The former was a gathering of both sexes for Bible study, prayer, and common concern. The itinerant preacher or circuit rider held these congregations together with proclamation and sacraments, but Methodist laity participated in the leadership of the small groups, carrying out the day-to-day ministry of the local congregation as the minister moved on to another distant charge.

Baptists also established methods of responding to frontier society. Indeed, in nineteenth-century America, perhaps no group exemplified the concern for liberty and localism more than the people called Baptists. William Warren Sweet attributed the growth of the Baptists to four important factors: 1) simplicity of doctrine; 2) democratic polity; 3) propagation without bureaucracy; 4) and a strong popular appeal to the common folk due to doctrinal simplicity and democratic polity.[40] Sweet was particularly impressed with what he called the Baptist "Farmer-Preacher," a man of the people whose bi-vocational occupation placed him close to those to whom he ministered.[41] Sweet cited Theodore Roosevelt's comment that, "The Baptist preachers lived and worked exactly as their flocks . . . they cleared the ground, split rails, planted corn, and raised hogs on equal terms with their parishioners."[42] These farmer-preachers were often uneducated or self-educated. They testified to a divine call and were ordained by the autonomous Baptist congregations they served without the sanction of presbytery, synod or bishop.

Nineteenth-century Baptist churches often served as sources of law and order in the frontier environment of the American West. Protestant congregations often exercised strenuous discipline over their membership, responding to such social and moral issues as

[40]William Warren Sweet, *Religion and the Development of American Culture* (New York: Charles Scribner's Sons, 1952) 110.
[41]Ibid., 111.
[42]Ibid., citing Theodore Roosevelt, *The Winning of the West*, NY, 1900, III, 101.

robbery, murder, gambling, alcohol, sexual immorality, and abuse of slaves, spouses or children. Contrary to contemporary stereotypes, Protestant opposition to alcohol was due less to prudery than to serious social concern. Alcohol was condemned for its influence on poverty, family abuse, immorality and idleness.[43] Sweet concludes that, "Self-reliance, courage, the spirit of freedom and adventure, stanch and rugged individualism, and the democratic spirit—all were nourished in the west. But all of these fine qualities and characteristics, born of the frontier, would have gone for naught had there not been planted in the far flung communities of the west the seeds of moral, spiritual and cultural life."[44]

In this setting, competition between Protestant denominations flourished. With disestablishment and religious freedom, churches were forced to compete for members who would choose to support one denomination or another. One important source of authority centered in the claim to primitivism, that effort to establish a particular tradition—Baptist, Methodist, Presbyterian, or Restorationist—as closest to the Churches of the New Testament. Old Landmarkism was one effort to claim primitivism from a Baptist perspective. Landmarkists insisted that they were founded, not by Luther, Calvin, Zwingli, or Cranmer, but on Jesus as baptized by John. Unlike the "Disciples" or followers of Alexander Campbell, Baptists had no need to "restore" New Testament Christianity, since they had never lost it in the first place. It had been kept alive by landmark Churches since the time of the apostles. These Churches—Montanist, Paulician, Cathari, Waldensian, Anabaptist, and others—ran like a "trail of blood" and martyrs across the pages of history. The true Church was the Church of the persecuted and the oppressed.

The name, Old Landmark, was taken from Proverbs 22, "Remove not the ancient Landmarks which thy fathers hath set." The word was used as early as 1854 by J. M. Pendleton, pastor of First Baptist Church, Bowling Green, Kentucky. That year Pendleton published an essay addressing the question, "Ought Baptists to recognize Pedo-baptist (infant baptizer) preachers as gospel ministers?" Pendleton's work, written at the request of J. R. Graves of Nashville, Tennessee, was entitled *An Old Landmark ReSet*. It

[43]Ibid., 140.
[44]Ibid., 137.

was the first of numerous treatises written over the next decade by Pendleton, Graves, and other adherents of the Landmark ecclesiology. Their views on the nature of the Church and democratic idealism bear some striking parallels with certain liberationist concepts regarding basic Christian communities or Peoples' Churches.

In a work entitled *Distinctive Principles of Baptists*, J. M. Pendleton wrote that, "A scriptural church is a local congregation of baptized believers independent, under Christ, of the state and of every other church, having itself authority to do whatever a church can of right do."[45] Local Baptist churches were independent of each other but united in common doctrine and fellowship. For Pendleton and other Landmarkers, every local congregation "is as complete a church as ever existed, and is perfectly competent to do whatever a church can of right do." "It is as complete as if it were the only church in the world."[46] Each congregation contained within itself the complete elements of the one true Church.

Decision-making in these churches was based in the Christian community utilizing democratic polity. Pendleton declared that, "Churches are executive democracies organized to carry out the sovereign will of their Lord and King."[47] Christ's authority was mediated through the community of believers. To say that Christ was Head of the Church was to speak in terms of monarchy, true enough. Yet Christ's kingdom, "in its organized state of small communities, each managing its own affairs in its own vicinage, is a pure democracy."[48] In the true Church, therefore, "THE PEOPLE—THE WHOLE PEOPLE—in each community choose their own officers, receive and expel members, conduct all business as a body politic, decide on all questions of discipline, and observe all the institutions of Christ."[49] Each church chose its own officers/ministers—pastors and deacons. They could do nothing apart from the consent of the church's members. No congrega-

---

[45]J. M. Pendleton, *Distinctive Principles of Baptists*, (Philadelphia: American Baptist Publication Society, 1882) 169. For a description of the history of Landmarkism see Leon McBeth, *The Baptist Heritage* (Nashville: Broadman Press, 1987) 447–61.

[46]Ibid., 186.

[47]Ibid., 187.

[48]Ibid.

[49]Ibid.

tion could select the officers and leaders of any other local congregation.[50]

This democratic form of Peoples' Church had at last come of age in the world and was the sign of the future. Pendleton observed that, "Oppressed humanity, under the burdens imposed by monarchy and aristocracy, is everywhere restless and waiting for a suitable opportunity to assert its rights."[51] The people were rising up to receive the gospel and democracy as well. Pendleton wrote optimistically that the people were discovering themselves as the "source of power." He noted that while it was impossible to say how much independence and freedom in the Church had influenced the idea in society, there was every reason to suppose that it promoted such freedom.[52]

The democratic nature of the church meant that it was also important for discipline to be maintained. Church members were responsible for one another even when correction from wrong was necessary. Like other frontier congregations, Landmark churches did not hesitate to "exclude" those whose orthodoxy and orthopraxy did not measure up to the demands of Scripture and community.

Landmarkism was also a way in which Baptists could establish their own form of catholicity among the evident pluralism of nineteenth-century American Protestant sects. J. R. Graves' delineation of the "marks" of the Church gives evidence of his almost obsessive concern for the local nature of basic Christian communities. Graves was perhaps the best known of the Landmark leaders whose polemical attitudes made him the most controversial spokesman of the movement. His struggle with non-Landmark Baptists produced great divisions in the Baptist ranks. These "marks" include:

1) For J. R. Graves, "The church and kingdom of Christ is a Divine institution."[53] The kingdom of Christ was inseparable from the local congregation of believers.

---

[50]Ibid., 199.

[51]Ibid., 213.

[52]Ibid., 213–14.

[53]J. R. Graves, *Old Landmarkism: What Is It?* (Ashland, KY: Calvary Baptist Church Book Shop, 1880) 26.

2) The church "is a visible institution."[54] Graves believed that "the only church that is revealed to us is a visible church. . . ."[55] The universal Church simply did not exist in Scripture or history, Graves declared.

3) The church's "locality is upon earth."[56] Graves concluded that "the locality of Christ's church, and therefore kingdom, is this earth; all the subjects of His kingdom are here; all the work of His church is here."[57]

4) The church is "a local organization, a single congregation." Both Graves and Pendleton repudiated the idea of a universal, national or provincial Church. For them the New Testament use of the word *ekklesia* applied only to a local entity.[58] Each local cell received from Christ the authority to proclaim the gospel and administer the sacraments/ordinances of baptism and the Lord's Supper.

5) "The membership (of the church) all professedly regenerate in heart before baptized into it."[59] Landmarkism thus stands within the tradition of a believer's church. Faith in Christ was the foundation for entrance into the Body of Christ. With other Baptists, Landmarkists rejected the idea and practice of infant baptism in favor of the total immersion of those who could testify to personal faith in Christ.

6) The church's "baptism is the profession, on the part of the subject, of the faith of the Gospel by which he is saved."[60] Baptism, therefore, is "an act by which we profess the saving faith we possess. . . ."[61]

7) The Lord's Supper is itself "a local church ordinance, commemorative only of the sacrificial chastisement of Christ for his people. . . . [62] Each church, Graves believed, was the "guardian" of the Supper. Thus participation in the Lord's Supper was closely related to the disciplinary task of the church. This view, sometimes known as "close communion," meant that only members of a lo-

[54]Ibid., 27.
[55]Ibid., 28.
[56]Ibid.
[57]Ibid., 29.
[58]Ibid., 32.
[59]Ibid., 41.
[60]Ibid., 48.
[61]Ibid., 57.
[62]Ibid., 58; and J. M. Pendleton, *Christian Doctrines* (Philadelphia: American Baptist Pub. Soc., 1878) 342-57.

cal congregation could receive the Supper when it was celebrated in their church alone. Only bona fide members of a local community of faith could receive the Supper when it was celebrated there. This ordinance, as Graves called it, was a "simple memorial of Christ's work and love for us. . . ."[63] It was not a "sacrament" or a "seal" aimed at securing "conversion, justification, or remission of sins. . . ."[64]

At the same time, Old Landmarkists were not Quakers, promoting only the ministry of the laity. They accepted an ordained ministry, called out by God. Yet they asserted, in Graves' words, that "the preaching of the gospel, and administering of the ordinances, belong strictly to a specific officer of a local church—can only be done by its authority and under its guardianship."[65] Ministerial authority came only through Christ as mediated by the local congregation.

Pendleton noted that "the power of the church cannot be delegated."[66] He cited Acts 15:22-23 as evidence that the entire church, "the brethren," were named "in connection with the 'apostles and elders' " as possessing authority for the guidance of the church.[67]

In one sense, Landmark leaders such as Graves and Pendleton sound somewhat apolitical, promoting certain "spiritual" concerns of personal evangelism, moralism, and theological speculation. Yet they were also captivated by the democratic idealism which permeated nineteenth-century American Protestantism. If liberation theologians might be accused of looking to Marxism or socialism as a political guide for basic communities and response to the poor, Landmarkists and other Protestants might be accused of a naivete regarding the benefits of democracy. In a remarkable little volume called *The Watchman's Reply*, published in 1853, J. R. Graves identified Baptists with the "poor" and "oppressed" of the world, a people persecuted by Protestant and Catholic establishments alike. He saw the rise of "popular revolutions" around the world as evidence of the triumph of democracy and true Christianity over

---

[63]Ibid., 68; and Pendleton, *Christian Doctrines*, 358–67.

[64]Ibid.

[65]Ibid., 97.

[66]J. M. Pendleton, *Three Reasons, Why I Am A Baptist* (Cincinnati: Moore, Anderson and Company, 1853) 153.

[67]Ibid.

"tyranny and caste."[68] He wrote that the "religion of Christ binds kingly and clerical despots in bonds and cords, that the people may be left free, and the Word of God run and be glorified, and its ennobling and regenerating principles may permeate the masses of humanity and redeem a lost race to God."[69]

Like many nineteenth-century Americans, Graves saw the new nation as the chosen vehicle of the deliverance of the race. "Here," he wrote, "is Paradise regained—man [*sic*] is restored to the full enjoyment of all his lost rights—emancipated from every foe but sin. . . ."[70] America offered the world the twin blessing of "Republicanism and Christianity." These blessings were purchased with blood, not only that shed in the American Revolution, but also "of the precious blood of Him who died on Calvary."[71]

Churches of Christ, therefore, were "pure democracies," "the sole gift of the Gospel" to humanity.[72] The democracy of the church was the model and mirror for democracy in the state. Thus the gospel was the source of true liberation, both spiritual and political. Christianity was the source of freedom for all the people. Graves wrote of this liberating gospel:

> The religion of Christ constitutes the *people*, the foundation of all power, and establishes and protects their *supreme sovereignty*. The Gospel gives them a charter, written by God, to protect them against the tyranny of the political usurper, and the still more dreadful despotism of the spiritual ruler and lordling in the church—in a word it teaches (as never man [*sic*] before taught) us all, not only that we *may* be free, but that it is *our imperative duty*, as Jesus Christ's freeman—to be free indeed, and to think and act politically and religiously for ourselves. . . .[73]

Like other Baptists before him, J. R. Graves insisted that religious liberty was the hallmark of civil liberty. If it was true that "like priest, like people," it was also true that "like religion, like government."[74] Hierarchy in Church or government created a serf-like populace. This was particularly evident in countries dominated

---

[68] J. R. Graves, *The Watchman's Reply* (Nashville: Graves and Shankland, 1853) 11.
[69] Ibid., 13.
[70] Ibid., 14.
[71] Ibid., 15.
[72] Ibid., 16.
[73] Ibid., 16–17.
[74] Ibid., 18.

by Romanism or "Protestant sects." The choice was simple for such Protestant establishments: they could become Catholic or Baptist, establishment or liberationist![75]

Graves saw in the American Revolution the beginning of a world-wide burst of freedom and liberation. He wrote that, "By civil revolutions alone will God prepare the nations for the gospel, and I believe they are at hand."[76] He acknowledged, for example, that China was "revolutionizing," while Burma had been opened "by English arms."[77] He noted that, "A naval force is now crossing the ocean to open, *peaceably* or *forcibly*, the island empire of Japan, and all Europe is confessedly upon the eve of a revolution."[78] The "spirit of freedom" was "in full tide," sweeping across the globe.[79] Today's imperialism was yesterday's promise of freedom, at least where these Landmark writers were concerned. Democracy should be achieved and the oppressed liberated, even if by force of arms.

Graves continually warned his readers to be on guard against "kingcraft," "priestcraft," and hierarchies—particularly those represented in the Roman Catholic Church. He called upon "young America" to "oppose the prevalence of religious Hierarchism."[80] In this effort to bring "the whole empire in the west under the influence of *primitive republican* Christianity," more laborers were needed desperately.[81]

He wrote passionately: "Remember, young men, that *popular* or *democratic church government* is the great, if not the only guarantee to the perpetuity of democracy in the state."[82] Graves insisted that this liberty must be protected, since "just so long as parity and universal suffrage is triumphant in the churches of Christ, so long will it be in the state and NO LONGER!"[83] He manifested unfailing confidence in democracy in both the congregation and in the nation. He was convinced that the liberating power of

[75]Ibid., 59.
[76]Ibid., 58; and J. R. Graves, *The Tri-lemma* (Nashville: South-Western Publishing House, 1860) 119–51.
[77]Ibid.
[78]Ibid.
[79]Ibid.
[80]Ibid., 67.
[81]Ibid., 70.
[82]Ibid.
[83]Ibid.

democracy was set to prevail on the world, and that the agents of gospel democracy must work unceasingly to overcome the old establishment autocracy in the Church and the world. He saw himself and his movement as rising up from the world's oppressed, those long persecuted for freedom and the gospel's sake. Now the yoke was cast off and the long-awaited liberation had begun.

Unlike the advocates of base ecclesial communities, neither Graves nor Pendleton gave extensive attention to the plight of the poor. Pendleton does have at least two published sermons which address the issue of riches relative to Christians. In one sermon entitled "The Rich Saved with the Greatest Difficulty," Pendleton declared that, "It is not desirable to be rich. The possession of a competency (adequacy) is decidedly preferable."[84] He warned that persons became rich at the expense of the poor. "The necessities of the unfortunate are frequently allowed to open the way to the attainment of wealth."[85] Riches distract sinners from reliance on Christ. "Their trust in riches excludes the Savior as the object of their faith. This trust in riches as infallibly prevents the salvation of the soul as does reliance on self-righteousness."[86] Pendleton was also careful to instruct those who had wealth in ways which that resource should be used for the relief of the poor and the upbuilding of the kingdom of God.[87]

Were Old Landmarkers promoting a nineteenth-century version of liberation theology? Of course they were not. Landmark obsession with local church autonomy kept them from recognizing the communal and universal nature of the Body of Christ. In their effort to interpret the word *ekklesia* as applied only to the local congregation, they overlooked the significance of such powerful Pauline metaphors as People of God, Community of Faith, and Body of Christ—evidence of the universal nature of the Church. Liberation theology has not made such a mistake.

Likewise, Landmark polemicism and claims to be the only true Church perpetuated competition among Christian denominations

[84]J. M. Pendleton, *Short Sermons on Important Subjects* (St. Louis: National Baptist Publishing Company, 1859) 371.

[85]Ibid., 373.

[86]Ibid., 380.

[87]Ibid., 381–95. Graves tended to spiritualize the rich man and Lazarus in J. R. Graves, *The Dispensational Expositions of the Parables and Prophecies of Christ* (Memphis: Graves and Mahaffy, 1887) 216–36.

and evolved into its own type of establishment within the Baptist tradition. Their sincere efforts to maintain Church discipline often deteriorated into petty bickering and political intrigue in the name of Christian orthodoxy. In addition, the Landmarkists' optimism over the benefits of American democracy often failed to anticipate its imperialistic side.

Yet both liberation theology and Old Landmarkism reflect a radical reassertion of the importance of the local congregation and the role of the people as a source of authority and ministry for the whole Church. Both represent a profound response to hierarchies and establishments which, knowingly or unknowingly, undermine the importance of the individual believer and congregation in the decision-making role and missionary imperative of the Church. In their own unique ways, both remind the Church that the salvation it proclaims and the sacraments it offers cannot be understood and appropriated apart from community. If Landmarkists pushed localism too far in rejecting any idea of the universal nature of the Church, that does not negate their contribution in seeking to renew the Church's grass-roots identity. Both liberation theology and Old Landmarkism represent a reassertion of the mission and ministry of the local congregation. Could base ecclesial communities, or at least some of them, press localism to the limits, rejecting the traditional ecclesial structures as corrupted beyond redemption?

Both were and are products of their time in the optimistic assessment they often maintain toward certain political/economic ideologies. Landmarkism saw democracy as the vehicle of liberation for nineteenth-century society long shackled by the monarchies and autocracies of European dominance. If they were overly optimistic about American democracy as a vehicle for liberation world wide, they nonetheless anticipated a new day of hope for oppressed peoples. So liberation theology anticipates a new era of economic and political freedom which democratic socialism may help the oppressed in Latin America to realize. If they have been naive in some of their political speculations, they have nonetheless provided prophetic insight as to the necessity, indeed the inevitability, of reform from the dominance of militaristic dictatorships and economic exploitation. Landmarkists no doubt saw themselves as having been liberated from tyranny through democratic revolution and biblical religion. Liberationists see themselves as participating in the process of liberation, a liberation still on the way, not yet secured. Both movements recognized that they were living in a new day for the Church and the culture, a time of significant religious and political transition and, they hoped, renewal.

Finally, both movements call the Church to struggle with questions of salvation as heard in every age through the liberating word of Holy Scripture. Landmarkism and liberationism remind the Church that the people can be trusted in the reading and interpretation of the Bible. Landmarkists no less than liberationists read their own lives and experiences in the stories of the early Christian communities. Liberationists no less than Landmarkists see their baptism as representation of and participation in that liberating faith which stretches all the way from river Jordan to the rural churches of frontier North America and impoverished Latin America. In their respective contexts they sought to rediscover the truth of Scripture in the local community of faith. Until it is discovered there, with the persecuted and the poor—those long outside the religious establishment—faith can have no real meaning for the one true Church apostolic and universal.

Epilogue

Donald W. Dayton

I was delighted and honored to be asked to contribute an "epilogue" to this book which struggles with issues that have been puzzling me for some twenty years since the research for my *Discovering an Evangelical Heritage*.[1] In that book I explored some of the radical Protestant traditions for anticipations to modern currents like the civil rights movement, but also for parallels to certain features of the then emerging "liberation theology," especially its doctrine of the "preferential option for the poor." Since writing that book, I have continued to ponder the meaning of the sorts of phenomena that are explored in the present volume—and the more that I have thought about these things, the more my thinking has changed about a number of topics. I believe, therefore, that the present book makes a very important contribution; and if we would take this material seriously, it would revolutionize our thinking about a number of issues. I would like to use this short epilogue to attempt to raise some of those issues and to suggest some of the lines of rethinking and reinterpretation that would be called for.

In the first place, I think that the number of "case studies" like those explored in this book could be greatly extended. There are many other movements in the broader Wesleyan tradition that articulate a "preferential option for the poor"—the Church of the Nazarene, whose name was adopted to emphasize the "Jesus of the poor"; the Salvation Army, whose turn to the poor produced much similar rhetoric; other branches of the "holiness movement"

---

[1] *Discovering an Evangelical Heritage* (San Francisco: Harper and Row, 1976—revised edition Peabody, Massachusetts: Hendrickson, 1988), especially chapter nine, "Anointed to Preach the Gospel to the Poor."

where this theme often played a key role; and so on. In my book I explored similar movements among the Presbyterians, especially the currents associated with evangelist Charles Grandison Finney whose churches in New York were known as "free churches" because of their commitment to "free pews" in a way similar to the Free Methodists. Late in the nineteenth century Presbyterian A. B. Simpson was led by similar concerns to establish the Christian and Missionary Alliance. I had neglected the Campbellites and Baptists in my book and am fascinated with the studies of these traditions presented here. But especially important for the Latin American context is the great variety of Pentecostal movements which have come in recent years to dominate Protestantism south of the border—and often similar themes can be found in the literature of these movements.[2]

I have wondered also if the thesis of this book ought not to be radicalized. I share the concern of the contributors that some of these parallels should not be overdrawn—and that in most cases these movements were not full anticipations of "liberation theology" in that they were usually pre-Marxist or pre-modern in their social analysis, did not always move as directly to political action, and so forth. But I think that it is also true that we are so blinded by inadequate and inherited categories of thought that we are not able to see and understand the genuine radicalism of some of these antecedents to themes of modern "liberation theology." Let me then turn to some of the reorientations to which I have been led.

The issues in this book were highlighted recently in my work with a young Venezuelan student in my institution's "hispanic program." He was in the process of writing an essay to become part of a book interpreting the nature of the Protestant experience in his country. Influenced by "liberationist" themes, he was inclined to critique the cultural, economic, and religious "dependency" of his region on North Atlantic cultures in a search for "liberation" from "dominance" from the North. In the process we got into quite a debate about the nature of the Protestantism that the missionaries brought from the North and the extent to which it was

---

[2]This is becoming clear in recent literature on Pentecostalism—a fact that has often been stressed in various writings of Walter J. Hollenweger. For an illustration of this in the very earliest literature of Pentecostalism, see the preface of Cecil M. Robeck, Jr., to Frank Bartleman, *Witness to Pentecost* (New York: Garland, 1984).

a carrier of a form of "neo-imperialism" that stands in the line of "manifest destiny" thinking that grants to North America a "divine right" to extend its religious life to the rest of the world—a theme very prominent in the earliest waves of Protestant missionizing in the early nineteenth century. He appealed to the work of another of his teachers who had explored the thinking of the North American "social gospel" tradition to discover that even this—the supposedly most "liberal" strand of the North American churches—was permeated by a doctrine of "manifest destiny" that supported a form of "neo-imperialism." By definition, he argued then, all other more "conservative" traditions are also to be so characterized, and he was justified in analyzing *all* North American Christian missionary traditions from this point of view.

I argued that this was much too simplistic an analysis and that the "social gospel" was a form of "liberalism" that was still at the center of the culture and a carrier of its deepest values—in this sense still very "conservative" and "traditional." I suggested that he would find a much more radical rejection of the values of North American culture in more marginal religious movements—precisely those movements that have been most influential in the Protestant missionizing of Latin America and the shaping of Venezuelan Protestantism, for example. At the center of such discussion would be questions about how to interpret the significance of the rise of the eschatologically oriented movement of "dispensational premillennialism" that dominates Latin American Protestantism. This movement, at least *theoretically,* involves a very fundamental rejection of the "manifest destiny" themes that are part and parcel of the "post-millennial" eschatology offering the hope of a gradual spread of the "civilizing" work of the traditionally Protestant cultures toward a utopian end of history. And again *consistently,* such a theology should condemn the United States and its government as a part of the decadence of this age under the powers of evil. Such theology can have profound political consequences—as it did in Japan during World War II when its advocates were imprisoned and executed because their theology implied that the Japanese emperor would be proven not to be "divine" when Christ returned to be revealed as the *true* "King of Kings and Lord of Lords."

Such facts at least hint at the inadequacy of many of the categories that we use to think about religious movements. We are conditioned to think in terms of a single spectrum of "conservative/liberal" along which we measure all traditions. In part this thinking is shaped in the twentieth century by the "fundamentalist/modernist" controversy and the "neo-fundamentalist" or "evangelical" apologetics and historiography that have convinced us that the movements that we often label today "evangelical" are more "traditional" or "conservative" or "orthodox" than those "liberal" movements of the mainstream that have supposedly capitulated to modernity. I am becoming more and more convinced that this "conservative/liberal" paradigm must be radically revised if not fundamentally rejected—and that many phenomena are better explained by a construct that moves in a very different and at times opposite direction.

The three case studies in this book (Landmark Baptists, Free Methodists, and the more radical Campbellites) are often included in the category "evangelical" and thus assumed to be "conservative"—and in some cases to be even benightedly "reactionary" and "conservative" in that their extremism positions them further away from the mainstream than the more "enlightened evangelicals." I think it would be better to describe these traditions as more "radical" in a way that would emphasize that far from being the carriers of an impulse to defend "traditional" Protestantism they are at their heart a rejection of "traditional" Protestantism in a way that even including them in the category of "Protestantism" may confuse the issue and mislead our thinking about their nature and impact. Once one raises this question, one begins to notice certain features (such as the rejection of more traditional ecclesiology and views of the sacraments and the ministry) that illustrate this point. Often the movement away from the center of the culture (often involving a movement toward the poor) provides the space for social experimentation outside the mainstream.

The need for this reorientation can perhaps be most clearly illustrated by the study of the ministry of women in the various churches. The "conservative/liberal" paradigm conditions us to think that the "liberal" churches of the cultural "mainstream" are the pioneers of the ministry of women—and that the "evangelicals" are those who resist this practice on traditional grounds. Actually, almost the opposite is the actual situation. The churches of the National Association of Evangelicals pioneered the ministry of women in the last century; the "mainstream" and "liberal" churches of the National Council of Churches began to embrace the ministry of women only in the middle of this century. Yet our dominant patterns of thinking often suppress such facts and prevent them from surfacing as useful bridges that might open up a more profound ecumenical discussion between these alienated parties.[3]

I am afraid that a similar phenomenon is happening in Latin America, where popular and dissenting forms of Protestantism are growing so fast that anthropologist David Stoll was able to write recently a widely-discussed book under the title *Is Latin America Turning Protestant?: The Politics of Evangelical Growth* (Berkeley: University of California Press, 1990). That book accepts much of the "conservative/liberal" paradigm and describes two ideologies competing for the "soul" of Latin America: "liberation theology" and a popular "evangelicalism" (most typically Pentecostalism). Stoll's statistics suggest that not only are several Latin American countries on the edge of slipping out from under traditional Roman Catholic hegemony but that these forms of Protestantism are outrunning in influence the various forms of "liberation theology" that from a distance we tend to associate with Latin American religious life.

Actually, the texture of Latin American Protestantism is not well understood—as I have come to see in participation in various aspects of the modern ecumenical movement over the last decade. This was made especially clear to me at the 1991 Canberra (Australia) assembly of the World Council of Churches. From a distance some think of the WCC as dominated by the Latin Americans and their discussion of "liberation theology." Closer to the truth is the fact that the Latin Americans are radically marginalized in such contexts—they were represented in Canberra by only about 20 delegates out of nearly a thousand. The reason for this is rather obvious once one has noticed the phenomenon. The Latin Ameri-

[3]I have explored these reorientations in a number of places, but probably most accessibly in "Yet Another Layer of the Onion; Or Opening the Ecumenical Door to Let the Riffraff In," *The Ecumenical Review* 40 (January, 1988) 87–110.

can religious scene is dominated by non-participants in the ecumenical movement—Roman Catholics on the one hand and "radical" Protestants on the other. Pentecostalism, for example, is probably a majority of Protestantism in almost all Latin American countries—followed by other movements like the holiness movement (in the line of the Free Methodists) and other manifestations of radical "evangelicalism." Our categories of analysis, shaped by the "conservative/liberal" paradigm, identify the Catholic tradition with "liberation theology" and incline us to think of the Protestants as representative of the most extremely "traditional" and "conservative" forms of that movement at their heart in fundamental opposition to "liberation theology."

The significance of this book, with its exploration of the "radical" tendencies of precisely the forms of Protestantism that tend to dominate the Latin American scene, is that it explodes the "conservative/liberal" paradigm and opens up the possibility of building new bridges between these competing ideologies that will so profoundly shape the future of that continent. Particularly emphasized in this book are the convergence of radical ecclesiologies and in the variety of "preferential options for the poor" that could be brought into dialogue. I would like to suggest that these proposals are not a wild straining at the facts that shows little real potential but the first timid steps toward a dialogue that could be extended and amplified—and that much of value is buried in these traditions that our categories of thinking preclude us from noticing.

Let me, in conclusion, extend this discussion by giving a few illustrations of other ways in which these traditions could be brought into dialogue with liberation theology. I've done much of my thinking in the analysis of Pentecostalism, and my comments will be shaped by my orientation toward that tradition.

(1) In some ways I think that the "preferential option for the poor" in B. T. Roberts may be in some ways more radical and more profoundly theologically grounded than in some forms of "liberation theology." Roberts makes "preaching the gospel to the poor" *essential* to the very messianic office of Jesus—and thus defining of ecclesiology and mission. The theme becomes the *sine qua non* by which one discerns a true church: "There are hot controversies about the true church . . . . It may be that there cannot be a church without a bishop, or that there can. There can be none

without a gospel, and a gospel to the poor.''[4]

(2) Closely associated with the radical ecclesiologies analyzed in this book is the radical, often experientially based, "gospel egalitarianism" that so powerfully attracts the poor by affirming their value apart from traditional hierarchies or the privileges of class, education, and so on. "Liberation theology" often claims to be a "church of the poor," but it sometimes has difficulty moving out of the Universities and other elite social locations to become genuinely a church of the poor. Some forms of "radical" Protestantism have found themselves moving more easily and naturally into the life of the poor—and may speak to real needs and may provide their own form of powerful conscientization that perhaps should be taken more seriously as models of social transformation. Here the history of the debate about the social impact of the rise of Methodism during the industrial revolution in the British context may prove instructive—as it is applied to the Latin American situation by David Martin in *Tongues of Fire: The Explosion of Protestantism in Latin America* (Oxford: Blackwell, 1990).

(3) Beneath the surface of the "pie in the sky" and other-worldly eschatologies that sometimes seem to dominate these forms of radical Protestantism are often world-affirming dimensions that could be used to develop some theological common ground. I have often pondered the extent to which the "divine healing" doctrines of the holiness and pentecostal movements are actually an affirmation of a salvific divine intention for the *body* and thus this world in a way that could be developed in a social and political direction into dialogue with various forms of "liberation theology." This insight found unexpected historical confirmation in my research on the history of the healing movement when I discovered that both this movement and the religious socialists of central Europe claim common roots in the same rediscovery by the Blumhardts (father and son) of an active, powerful presence of God to restore and reorder the fallen creation.[5]

[4]This quotation is taken from the editorial by Roberts in the first issue of his paper *The Earnest Christian*, the essay regularly cited in successive editions of the Free Methodist Church *Discipline*. It may also be found in my *Discovering an Evangelical Heritage*, p. 112.

[5]I've suggested some of this in my *Theological Roots of Pentecostalism* (Metuchen, NJ: Scarecrow Press, 1987; paperback edition by Hendrickson Publishers, 1991) in a chapter on the rise of the "healing movement."

Such suggestions could be extended, but perhaps this will suffice to indicate some of the ways in which this discussion could be extended—and indicate some of the reasons that I am profoundly thankful for the efforts in this book to open up these and related issues.

Bibliography

Annual Meetings: Proceedings of the Annual Conferences of the Free Methodist Church [serial] 1903, 1912, 1916.

Boff, Leonardo. *Church, Charism, and Power: Liberation Theology and the Institutional Church*. Trans. by John W. Dierchsmeier. New York: Crossroad, 1984.

_____. *Ecclesiogenesis: The Base Communities Reinvent the Church*. Trans. by Robert R. Barr. Maryknoll, NY: Orbis Books, 1986.

Boff, Leonardo, and Clodovis Boff. *Cómo hacer teología de la liberación*. Madrid: Ediciones Paulinas, 1986.

Boff, Leonardo, and Virgil Elizondo, ed. *The People of God Amidst the Poor*. Edinburgh: T. & T. Clark Ltd, 1984.

Bowen, Elias. *History of the Origin of the Free Methodist Church*. Rochester, NY: B. T. Roberts, 1871.

Brown, Robert McAfee. *Theology in a New Key: Responding to Liberation Themes*. Philadelphia: The Westminster Press, 1978.

Bureau of the Census, *Religious Bodies, 1906,* 2 vols. Washington, D. C.: Government Printing Office, 1910.

_____. *Religious Bodies, 1916,* 2 vols. Washington, D. C.: Government Printing Office, 1919.

Cardenal, Ernesto. *The Gospel in Solentiname*. Trans. by Donald D. Walsh. Maryknoll, NY: Orbis Books, 1976.

Carroll, H. K. *The Religious Forces of the United States*. New York: The Christian Literature Company, 1893.

Clissold, Stephen. *The Saints of South America*. London: Charles Knight & Co., 1972.

Conferencia del Episcopado Latinoamericano, *Documentos de Puebla*. Madrid: PPC, 1979.

Cross, Whitney R. *The Burned-Over District: A Social and Intellectual History of Enthusiastic Religion in Western New York, 1800–1850*. New York: Harper & Row Publishers, 1965.

Damon, Charles M. *Sketches and Incidents, or Reminiscences of Interest in the Life of the Author*. Chicago: Free Methodist Publishing House, 1900.

Dayton, Donald. *Discovering An Evangelical Heritage*. New York: Harper & Row Publishers, 1976.

_____. *Theological Roots of Pentecostalism*. Metuchen, NJ: Scarecrow Press, 1987.

_____. "Yet Another Layer of the Onion; Or Opening the Ecumenical Door to Let the Riffraff In." *The Ecumenical Review* 40 (January 1988) 87–110.

The Doctrine and Discipline of the Holiness Movement, or Church. Ottawa, ON: Holiness Movement Publishing House, 1907.

Eagleson, John, and Philip Scharper, eds. *Puebla and Beyond: Documentation and Commentary*. Trans. by John Drury. Maryknoll, NY: Orbis Books, 1979.

Earnest Christian [periodical] 1860, 1861, 1863, 1864, 1865, 1867, 1869, 1870, 1871, 1872, 1876.

Ferm, Deane William. *Third World Liberation Theologies: An Introductory Survey*. Maryknoll, NY: Orbis Books, 1986.

Ferm, Deane William, ed. *Third World Liberation Theologies: A Reader*. Maryknoll, NY: Orbis Books, 1986.

Free Methodist [periodical] 1916.

Gibellini, Rosino, ed. *Frontiers of Theology in Latin America*. Trans. by John Drury. Maryknoll, NY: Orbis Books, 1979.

González, Justo. *Faith and Wealth: A History of Early Christian Ideas on the Origin, Significance, and Use of Money*. San Francisco: Harper & Row, 1990.

_____. "Voices of Compassion." *Missiology* 20 (April 1992) 163–73.

Goodpasture, H. McKennie, ed. *Cross and Sword: An Eyewitness History of Christianity in Latin America*. Maryknoll, NY: Orbis Books, 1989.

The Gospel Advocate [periodical] 1866, 1867, 1868, 1869, 1870, 1873, 1889, 1892, 1897, 1904, 1908.

Graves, J. R. *Old Landmarkism: What Is It?* Ashland, KY: Calvary Baptist Church Book Shop, 1880.

_____. *The Tri-lemma*. Nashville: South-Western Publishing House, 1860.

_____. *The Watchman's Reply*. Nashville: Graves and Shankland, 1853.

Gutiérrez, Gustavo. *The Power of the Poor in History: Selected Writings*. Trans. by Robert R. Barr. Maryknoll, NY: Orbis Books, 1983.

_____. *A Theology of Liberation: History, Politics, and Salvation.* Trans. and ed. by Sister Caridad Inda and John Eagleson. Maryknoll, NY: Orbis Books, 1973.

Harrell, David Edwin, Jr. *A Social History of the Disciples of Christ*, vol. 1: *Quest for a Christian America: The Disciples of Christ and American Society to 1866.* Nashville: The Disciples of Christ Historical Society, 1966; vol. 2: *The Social Sources of Division in the Disciples of Christ, 1865–1900.* Atlanta and Athens, GA: Publishing Systems, Inc., 1973.

Hennelly, Alfred, ed. *Liberation Theology: A Documentary History*. Maryknoll, NY: Orbis Books, 1990.

Higgs, Robert. *The Transformation of the American Economy, 1865–1914: An Essay in Interpretation.* The Wiley Series in American Economic History. Ralph L. Andreano, ed. New York: John Wiley & Sons, Inc., 1971.

Hooper, Robert E. *Crying in the Wilderness: A Biography of David Lipscomb.* Nashville: David Lipscomb College, 1979.

Hughes, Richard T., Henry E. Webb, and Howard E. Short. *The Power of the Press: Studies of the Gospel Advocate, the Christian Standard, and The Christian-Evangelist.* The Forrest F. Reed Lectures for 1986. Nashville: The Disciples of Christ Historical Society, 1987.

Hynson, Leon O. *To Reform the Nation: Foundations of Wesley's Ethics.* Grand Rapids, MI: Francis Asbury Press, 1984.

Jennings, Theodore W., Jr. *Good News to the Poor: John Wesley's Evangelical Economics.* Nashville: Abingdon Press, 1990.

Lipscomb, David. *Civil Government: Its Origin, Mission, and Destiny, and the Christian's Relation to It.* Nashville: McQuiddy Printing Co., 1913.

Little, Lester. *Religious Poverty and the Profit Economy in Medieval Europe.* Ithaca, NY: Cornell University Press, 1978.

Lois, Julio. *Teología de la liberación: Opción por los pobres.* San José: Departamento Ecuménico de Investigaciones, 1986.

Magnuson, Norris. *Salvation in the Slums.* Metuchen, NJ: Scarecrow Press, 1977.

Marston, Leslie Ray. *From Age to Age a Living Witness: A Historical Interpretation of Free Methodism's First Century*. Winona Lake, IN: Light and Life Press, 1960.

Martin, David. *Tongues of Fire: The Explosion of Protestantism in Latin America*. Oxford: Blackwell, 1990.

Mathews, Lois Kimball. *The Expansion of New England: The Spread of New England Settlement and Institutions to the Mississippi River, 1620–1865*. Boston: Houghton Mifflin, 1909.

McBeth, Leon. *The Baptist Heritage*. Nashville: Broadman Press, 1987.

Mires, Fernando. *La colonización de las almas: Missión y conquista de América*. San José: Departamento Ecuménico de Investigaciones, 1987.

Mollat, Michel. *The Poor in the Middle Ages*. New Haven: Yale University Press, 1986.

Nugent, Walter T. K. *From Centennial to World War: American Society, 1876–1917*. The History of American Society. Jack P. Green, ed. Indianapolis: The Bobbs-Merrill Company, Inc., 1977.

Oblinger, Carl D. *Religious Mimesis: Social Bases for the Holiness Schism in Late Nineteenth Century Methodism*. Evanston, IL: Institute for the Study of American Religion, 1973.

L'Osservatore romano. 12 September 1962.

Owen, Olin M. *Rum, Rags, and Religion, or In Darkest America and the Way Out*. Buffalo, NY: A. W. Hall, 1893.

Pendleton, J. M. *Christian Doctrines*. American Baptist Publication Society, 1878.

———. *The Dispensational Expositions of the Parables and Prophecies of Christ*. Memphis: Graves and Mahaffy, 1887.

———. *Distinctive Principles of Baptists*. Philadelphia: American Baptist Publication Society, 1882.

———. *Short Sermons on Important Subjects*. St. Louis: National Baptist Publishing Company, 1859.

———. *Three Reasons, Why I Am a Baptist*. Cincinnati: Moore, Anderson and Company, 1853.

Persell, Caroline Hodges. *Understanding Society: An Introduction to Sociology*. New York: Harper & Row Publishers, 1984.

Robeck, Cecil M., Jr. Preface to *Witness to Pentecost*, by Frank Bartleman. New York: Garland, 1984.

Roberts, B. T. *Ordaining Women*. Rochester, NY: Earnest Christian Publication Co., 1891.

Roof, Wade Clark and William McKinney. *American Religion: Its Changing Shape and Future*. New Brunswick and London: Rutgers University Press, 1987.

Runyon, Theodore, ed. *Sanctification and Liberation: Liberation Theologies in the Light of the Wesleyan Tradition*. Nashville: Abingdon Press, 1981.

Second General Conference of Latin American Bishops. *The Church in the Present-Day Transformation of Latin America in the Light of the Council*. 2 vols. 2nd ed. Washington, D.C.: Division for Latin America, United States Catholic Conference, 1973.

Second Vatican Council, Decree on the Bishops' Pastoral Office in the Church, 28 October 1965.

_____. Decree on the Ministry and the Life of Priests, 7 December 1965.

_____. Dogmatic Constitution on the Church, 21 November 1964.

_____. Pastoral Constitution on the Church in the Modern World, 7 December 1965.

Shepherd, J. W., ed. *Queries and Answers by David Lipscomb*. 5th ed. Nashville: Gospel Advocate Company, 1963.

_____. *Salvation from Sin*. Nashville: Gospel Advocate Company, 1950.

Smith, Timothy L. *Revivalism and Social Reform*. New York: Abingdon Press, 1957.

Snyder, Howard A. *The Radical Wesley*. Downers Grove, IL: Inter-Varsity Press, 1979.

Sobrino, Jon. *The True Church and the Poor*. Trans. by Matthew J. O'Connell. Maryknoll, NY: Orbis Books, 1984.

Stoll, David. *Is Latin America Turning Protestant?: The Politics of Evangelical Growth*. Berkeley: University of California Press, 1990.

Storm, Roger C. *Partisan Prophets: A History of the Prohibition Party*. Denver: National Prohibition Foundation, 1972.

Sweet, William Warren. *Religion and the Development of American Culture*. New York: Charles Scribner's, 1952.

Tenney, Mary Alice. *Blueprint for a Christian World: An Analysis of the Wesleyan Way*. Winona Lake, IN: Light and Life Press, 1953.

_____. *Living in Two Worlds: How a Christian Does It!* Winona Lake, IN: Light and Life Press, 1959.

Walker, Williston, Richard A. Norris, David W. Lotz, and Robert T. Handy. *A History of the Christian Church.* 4th ed. New York: Charles Scribner's Sons, 1985.

West, Earl Irvin. *The Life and Times of David Lipscomb.* Henderson, TN: Religious Book Service, 1954.

Woodman, Harold D. "Sequel to Slavery: The New History Views the Postbellum South." *The Journal of Southern History.* 63 (4 [November 1977]).

Zahniser, Clarence Howard. *Earnest Christian: Life of Benjamin Titus Roberts.* Rochester, NY: By the Author, 1957.